Praise for *Finish Your Th* *Hacks for Success*

"This is an excellent guide to supporting you through your dissertation. I also love the coaching approach at the start of the book with the visualisation and goal setting. Not often I see this approach in academic literature and it sets this book apart from others I've seen. It is very clear that the author is highly experienced in supporting students through dissertations and this a very 'people centric' guide with guidance in all areas including a refreshing perspective on how to get the best out of your supervisor... extremely thorough and sensitively written; if you're about to start a dissertation this book is a MUST HAVE to see you through!"

Stephanie Rix, Career Coach and Founder of Life's Work Consulting.

"This is an excellent book, packed full of helpful advice and written in a clear and easy style. As a doctoral researcher I can see every section offers valuable insight, from first sitting down at the PC to final steps. Great value."

Jon Argent, Doctoral Researcher and Fellow of the Chartered Institute for the Management of Sport and Physical Activity.

"Known for his creative, inventive and accessible work, Professor Morrell has brought all of these qualities to bear on 'Finish Your Thesis'. It is a truly inventive book, written in an engaging style and packed full of very useful tips. The book is crammed with practical tips, broader insights and strategic gambits to bring a thesis / dissertation to a successful fruition. I strongly recommend this book. It will help."

Chris Carter, Professor of Strategy and Organization at the University of Edinburgh.

"The best of its kind. And the cheapest. A must-read for any dissertation student."

Jonathan Davies, Professor and founding Director of the Centre for Urban Research on Austerity.

Version 2.0 – now includes new sections on Stopping Procrastination, Myths on doing a Project, Additional sections on Trouble shooting, a Masterclass on doing an Upgrade (for PhD students), even quicker and easier to use with a streamlined structure, revised section on Understand Your Supervisor; also improved in response to feedback.

First published 2018 by Kindle

ASIN: B07DH96LFT

ISBN: 978-1-983-06921-5

© Kevin Morrell, 2018.

All Rights Reserved. This book or any portion thereof may not be reproduced or used in any manner whatsoever without the express written permission of the author except for fair dealing for the purposes of research or private study. It is permitted to use brief quotations in a book review under the terms of the Copyright, Designs and Patents Act 1988. For permission to reuse any material or any copyright queries contact the author by visiting www.kevin.morrell.org.uk

Disclaimer. The views expressed in this document are the author's alone and they do not reflect the views, policy or regulations of any institution or programme nor are they associated with any role. Under no circumstances is the author or publisher, or the author's employer(s) liable for any claim of indirect, incidental, consequential or special damages incurred by any person with respect to the advice offered here.

Contents

About the Author
Acknowledgements
A New Approach to Thesis Writing

Part 1: Hacks
Get the Most out of this Book
The Visualization Exercise
Habits and Routines
The What and the How
Timetables versus Milestones
Your Project is New and Different
Learn to Compartmentalise
Show Yourself who is Boss
Remember the Project is an Opportunity
Start with the End in Mind
Get the Perfect Structure in 7 Steps

Part 2: Tips
How to Do a Research Proposal
How To Choose a Topic
How To Choose Research Questions
Get an 'Eagle-eye View' of Your Project
Referencing and Citing other Work
Cite With Sophistication
Finding and Reading Articles
How to Use Google Scholar

Understand your Supervisor
Some Advice on Research Methods

Part 3: Writing Tips
How to Start
"Signposting" to help the Reader
Understanding Sentence Structure
Why Verbs beat Nouns
Should you Use "I" when Writing
Vocabulary Building - Describing Relationships
Layout and Presentation
If English is not your First Language

Part 4: Troubleshooting
4 Myths about Your Thesis or Dissertation
You left it Late to Start - Now what?
You are Struggling to get Access
You Haven't Got Enough Survey Responses
Your Interviewee Didn't Turn Up
Stop Procrastinating – Yes... You Can!
Major Changes: How to Tell Your Supervisor
Masterclass - 20 Examples of Successful Research
Masterclass For PhDs – Preparing for an Upgrade
Finish Your Thesis or Dissertation!

About the Author

Professor Kevin Morrell is Professor of Strategy at Durham University Business School where he is Director of the PhD programme and also Associate Dean for Postgraduate Research.

He has supervised hundreds of University projects at all levels, working at 5 UK Universities since gaining his PhD in 2002. He has authored and co-authored 5 books and published over 40 refereed articles in scientific journals in management studies, ethics, applied psychology, sociology and economics. In total he has over half a million words in print.

He holds a PhD from the University of Loughborough, Master's degrees from the Universities of Cambridge and Sheffield Hallam, and an Undergraduate degree from the University of Cambridge.

Kevin's website is www.kevin.morrell.org.uk he is also on LinkedIn www.linkedin.com/in/kevinmorrell and on Twitter @ProfKMorrell

Acknowledgements

Thanks to the following for their support and comments, the usual disclaimers apply:

Dr Hafez Abdo, Dr Barbara Allen, Professor Dimitris Assimakopoulos, Professor Linda Barton, Professor Chris Carter, Professor Jonathan Davies, Dr Rozana Huq, Professor Linda Kidwell, Dr Efrosyni Konstantinou, Professor Mark Learmonth, Steven Leuschel, Professor Tyrone Pitsis, Hari Ramaswamy, Dr Stephanie Scott, Dhanraj Singh, Dr Tracey Wond.

Images from Unsplash, thanks to: Tyler Nix, Brooke Lark, Chang Duong, Jacek Dylag, Lacie Slezak, Nikko Macaspac, Ramon Salinero, Raphael Biscaldi, Steve Harvye, Szucs Laszlo, Wil Stewart.

A New Approach to Thesis Writing

If you, or someone you care about, faces the challenge of doing a Thesis or Dissertation, this new book offers amazing *help and support*. As someone truly passionate about research, I wrote it to help people *avoid stress* and also because I want others to *enjoy and be inspired* to do their best work.

Often the phrase *work smarter* is a cliché but if you are doing a Thesis or Dissertation this can be a magical idea because this is exactly what the book is designed to do.

As a student, this book will help you to *maximize productivity* because it will help you *manage your time better* – to do what you need alongside your other commitments like applying for jobs or working or having a social life.

This practical manual is packed with advice - designed to help you instantly and inspire you to *succeed by yourself*. From cover to cover you will find hacks and tips. Hacks help you improve how you work, tips help you with what you work on.

It is based on 15 years of helping students from many nationalities, working at 5 Universities and supervising hundreds of people at all levels.

As an invited speaker at conferences and other Universities, and through print and online media, these hacks and tips have helped thousands more students to complete their projects. Now, by writing this book, *I can help you.*

Part 1: Hacks

"Give me six hours to chop down a tree and I will spend the first four sharpening the axe."

Abraham Lincoln

Get the Most out of this Book

Many of the hacks and tips in here are *very easy and quick to apply*. In fact, if you find something that you think is useful, my suggestion is that you try to use it right away and make some progress on your project. Then come back to the book later. If you can apply something straight away you will learn it better and you will be able to use it more easily on another occasion.

You do not need to read the whole book cover to cover to benefit from it. How it can be of most help to you will really depend on your needs and interests. You can read this book quickly end to end, or look at sections that most interest you, or look at areas where you think you will make the most improvement.

The very first exercise below is the only exception to this. I'm going to suggest it is required reading for anyone doing a Thesis or Dissertation. Even though it will feel strange and unfamiliar to do this exercise, please do not just skip it. Please take it seriously because it could help you more than any other tip or hack in the book.

Thank you for reading so far, please continue. *Enjoy the book.*

The Visualization Exercise

If you do this one exercise properly, it will repay the investment you have made in this book many times over. It will only take you a few minutes and it will also repay this small investment of time many times over (please have a pen and paper ready).

You can do this either before you get started, or when you are part-way through. As you progress through the project you can repeat this at any stage.

The two basic principles behind this exercise are very simple.

1. First, to be the most effective you can, you need to set goals.
2. Second, to work towards those goals effectively you need to have a clear picture of where you want to be.

Another way of expressing this is that it will help you to think of your future and where you want to be (successfully finishing your project) as a target that you aim for. You can't hit a target that you can't see clearly. This exercise helps you see this target clearly.

Ready? Here we go…

Try to visualise the following picture as clearly as you can. Please read it slowly. Make it real in your mind.

> Sitting alone in your room, you are feeling happy and proud. You just handed your work in 2 days before the deadline and you want to enjoy this moment because you know you did a good job.
>
> You left yourself with plenty of time to read through your final draft, then you had plenty of time to finish off the last stages before submission. You have done yourself justice. It is something you are very proud of and you also learned a lot along the way.
>
> You surprised yourself by becoming inspired and enjoying the work. Something you were anxious about turned out to be a great learning experience.
>
> You can see how the project and the skills you learned while doing it will be really valuable to you in future.

Please ... read the paragraphs above again more quickly and really try to visualise it once more. Think about your breathing while you are re-reading it. This will help you connect with an emotional state of feeling happy and proud and that in turn will make the picture clearer. Do this several times. I know this can feel strange but that doesn't matter, what matters is what you get out of this.

Remember the basic principles underpinning this exercise are to do with goal-setting. That end picture of you sitting in your room feeling happy and proud is your target. Now what we can do is take time to think about the journey you need to take from now – the time you are reading these words - to get to your imagined future target.

To do this you just need to answer the questions below. Spend some time on each question until you have *at least one thing* written down for each question.

- You must have worked reasonably hard - how did you reward yourself – healthily - for how you worked?

- What helped you to stay motivated?
- How did you find ways not just to work hard but to work smarter?
- You must have had some good routines - what routines helped you?
- What helped you to put regular, sustained effort in?
- You must have planned how to use your time effectively - how did you do that?
- To be effective, you must have developed some good habits - what were they?
- Like anyone doing this kind of project there were times when you felt like not working - how did you overcome these feelings quickly and not lose momentum?
- You must have made good use of the resources you had access to, both the visible and tangible ones and the less visible ones - what were these resources?

Now you have a target and you have started developing strategies to reach your target. You can return to this visualization exercise at any stage.

Habits and Routines

Alongside goals, a large part of success in these kinds of projects is having effective habits and routines. You are not stuck with the habits you have. The exciting thing about doing a Thesis or Dissertation is you can decide these things for yourself by starting afresh and if you treat it like a completely new project.

The origins of future habits lie in today's actions. To become habits, these actions simply get repeated. Starting today, why not make a decision to do a very few things well that will help you develop good habits over the course of your project?

The best place to start will be with deciding on a morning routine. This need only involve getting up at a certain time, being hydrated and having a healthy breakfast. You may also find it helpful doing a short, 3-minute meditation – so that you can start the day centred, which you could even try now (https://www.youtube.com/watch?v=rOne1P0TKL8). Right now, why not sketch out what your morning routine tomorrow will be?

Tomorrow I will get up at _ I will have _____ for breakfast and drink _____ glasses of water before doing a short meditation.

Often people's first reaction to these kinds of suggestions is to say they do not have time, but we are talking about something that could be done in 5-10 minutes, including 3 minutes meditating. It just means getting up 10 minutes earlier and this will repay itself over the course of the day.

Perhaps the thought of getting up slightly earlier or even at a set time makes you feel uncomfortable, but remember what Benjamin Franklin said "you will find the key to success under the alarm clock". As I will repeat later, the morning routine is important because when we can 'win' the morning we can also often win the day.

When you are starting out with doing a large academic project, you can start with the very end goal in mind, and you can also teach yourself at one level to think you have already finished. This means that you can work backwards to identify the habits and routines that will take you to that point.

This is a tactic a lot of extremely successful people use in life, from business people to sports stars, from musicians to other celebrities. You're not a celebrity yet, but the good news for you is this technique should be easier for you to use.

In life, one of the hardest challenges is knowing what goals to set yourself. Another challenge is you often don't know when something is finished. But you should have a clear idea of these things when doing an academic project – at least if you think about it in 'headline' terms. You know you need to hand in a project done to the best of your ability before a certain date.

That makes it easier for you to use things like the visualization technique. You already have a very specific goal set for you. Also, you know when you've finished – when you've handed in your work.

Let's come on to a phrase you will have heard many times before. This is the difference between "working harder" and "working smarter". This book is all about helping you work smarter.

But how do you work smarter?

Setting goals and developing effective habits and routines is key but there is a lot more you can do.

The What and the How

Here is one of the easiest and also most powerful hacks I use when helping people. It involves being aware of basic differences that a lot of people never stop to consider.

Don't just think about WHAT you must do.

Really reflect on HOW you do it.

The WHAT is what is in the final document - the introduction, literature review, methods, findings and analysis (if you must do these sections), discussion and conclusion.

The HOW involves thinking about how you plan, how you write these sections, how you carry out a literature review, how you work most effectively, how you make best use of time.

In my experience, unless they are explicitly encouraged to do so, few people ever stop to give HOW questions much thought. In general what happens is they think they have an idea of what they need to do, then they do it. Whatever planning people do is often just as simple as connecting two things:

(1) how many hours they are going to spend working
(2) what they are going work on

For instance – "I'm going to spend a whole day on my literature review". Or they might have a Gantt chart (a graph showing activities and time allocated to those).

That must be good right?

Well of course spending a day working is better than not doing any work. Naturally too, planning when you will spend time on different activities is better than not doing any planning. But you can do much better than this.

If you did the first exercise you are already further along than many people would be.

If you were to flick back to those questions you will see they are *all* about process. That is because by thinking about process you can work smarter.

Everyone at your institution is going to have to meet the same requirements in terms of WHAT they do. But no two people will work in the same way.

Some people will get up, stumble out of bed and drift into a day they spend stuck in front of a PC screen. They will work in the way cows graze.

Typing at the same time as looking at their phone they will be continually distracted by emails and social media.

If this sounds at all like you then you need to know this is not good. Seriously! You need to change this habit to work smarter.

Otherwise, you will not be as effective as if you – to take one example - took just two or three minutes to plan the day and then the same time at the end to review the day.

There is good news if you work in graze-mode. You can make some very simple changes now that will help you to some radical improvements very quickly.

Wouldn't you like to spend less time on your studies and be more effective? You can. A section later, on developing good habits can help you with this.

In my experience, one of the biggest reasons people do not finish as quickly as they could is they do not give enough attention to HOW they work.

By reading this book, you are pushing yourself ahead of most people.

That is because many, many people just "start" and carry on without ever giving thought as to how they can be most effective.

Here are things they never actively consider:

- how and when to plan the use of their time
- what their ultimate goals are - in detail
- what intermediate goals will help realise those ultimate goals
- what times of day they are most productive
- how to really focus
- how long they can focus for
- how often they should take breaks
- how they should recharge

- health, nutrition and exercise
- how they should stay committed and motivated
- what models of success they can follow.

Once you start thinking about these things you will force yourself to work smarter.

Let's come onto a second really simple and also fundamental hack.

Timetables versus Milestones

The timetable is an institutional requirement that must apply equally to ALL students (and faculty).

Milestones are the major goals in YOUR journey - key markers of progress that are specific to you and your project.

Don't confuse your milestones with the timetable.

A timetable might say:

- when you should be allocated a supervisor by
- when you should hand in a proposal
- when to do a first draft
- when you should hand in a final version of your work
- when you get your mark
- there might also be some classes or workshops meant to help you with your project.

Your milestones are very different.

These might be:

- decide on a topic
- have a constructive first meeting with your supervisor
- do a proposal then an extended proposal
- find an article that you think could be the basis for your whole project
- finish the first draft of the literature review
- arrange the first interview or finish the first version of your survey
- finish your discussion chapter and so on.

If the timetable says you must hand in a proposal after 3 weeks, there is nothing to stop you doing that AND writing 1,000 words of your review or even doing more.

You have no choice other than to respect the timetable. However, if you let the timetable dictate your pace this is a mistake. One reason is you might think you are on track but then you get blown off course – you lose data, you have a personal crisis and so on.

Remember the opening visualisation, where you finished 2 days before deadline?

That was picking a milestone of when you chose to hand in your final work. That milestone came 2 days before the timetabled deadline.

Imagine how much better is it to be in that position than to be running around stressed on the final day or working until 3 in the morning the night before. It is much better, right?

It's not even hard to do this. If you were to bring things forward by two days over the entire time you have for this project, it is not very much.

Try to imagine this: the deadline you have been given is the 12th of the month (let's say it's a Friday). They could just as easily have said it was that Wednesday the 10th couldn't they? So why not finish on the 10th?

Of course ... first make sure you have the right date for the deadline.

Also make sure right from the beginning you fully understand - from official sources - things like wordcount, format and requirements for the finished document.

Never rely on other students to tell you the answers to questions like that.

Let's consider for a minute why doing a Dissertation or Thesis is new and different.

Your Project is New and Different

By this stage of your career as a student you will have spent a lot of time in formal education. You might think by this stage you know what studying is all about.

But that could be a big mistake because whilst you may be a very effective student and learner, you may well need to develop different skills for this project.

Don't fall into the trap of thinking you already know how to "study" or even "write" because you will miss an opportunity to be more effective and efficient.

Why this is New

This will be a longer, bigger piece of work than you've done before. There may be some classes or workshops to support you, but there often aren't going to be lectures directly related to what you are doing.

It's a much more independent project and for the same reason you're also doing something different from your fellow students. In that sense, you are also disconnected from other students.

One positive way in which you are still a student of course is this still represents a great opportunity to learn about something in depth.

You may not get the time in your life again to focus on one question like this – and it's often a question you get to choose yourself.

As I'll show you later this could really help you with your career or in a job interview.

So: stop thinking about this as "part of your degree", or as if it means you are "coming to the end" of your degree, or as if it's "the last thing".

These things are true, but it is important to see they can trick you into not developing new habits and new ways of being effective.

Whilst it involves some of the same skills and subject knowledge, it is much more helpful to think this: This is different from anything you have done before.

It involves changes in your study routines, changes in how you learn and write, and it is a much longer project with different stages, that involves working alone more.

Because of this it is a great opportunity to step up.

Take the Opportunity to Develop Good Habits

A lot of people stumble into the beginning of the day. They get up, get dressed (maybe), have breakfast (maybe) turn on their laptop or PC and start work. This is what I called graze-mode earlier.

If you want to be efficient and this sounds like you, these are bad habits that you need to break.

That is easier to do if you start by thinking that this is a wholly new phase of your career as a student – as if it is almost like starting a new job.

Think about the first things you do in the morning. Do you drink a large glass of water? If not, that is a very easy new habit to start. It really affects your alertness and ability to concentrate if you are not hydrated.

Do you take time to have a healthy and nutritious breakfast? There is another easy new habit.

Think about when you turn on your laptop or PC. Do you start by checking Facebook, Twitter, Instagram, then check your email and then after these things are out of the way "start work"? Trust me, this is such a bad strategy.

To be effective, the first thing you need to do is plan for the day. Does this all make sense? You know all this.

Great – but in fact, you should start even earlier. The night before, write down a plan of what you want to achieve the next day.

Part of you will be thinking how to achieve this and when you wake up you will have a clear sense of direction first thing.

Try to "win the morning". If your morning goes well, you can "win the day".

What's it Really Like Doing a Dissertation or Thesis?

One hack that helps people is being prepared for a process that can be stressful and unpredictable.

In some books you see the process shown like this:

choose a topic

literature review

define research questions

collect data

data analysis

findings and discussion of data

implications of findings

conclusion

Some people find that helpful. But it is far from realistic in terms of preparing you. Here is what the journey is more like:

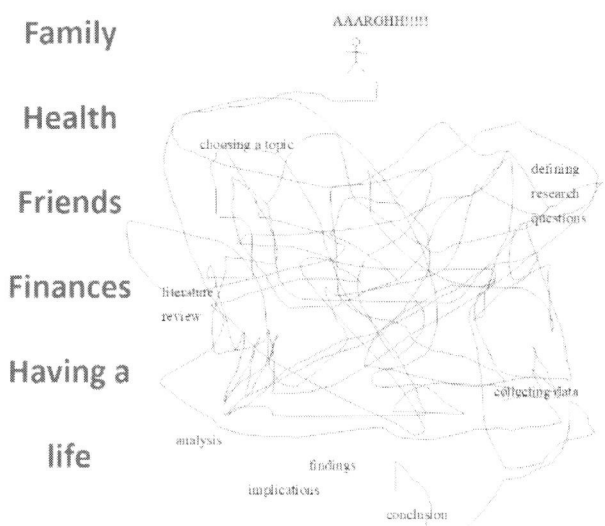

These include the same steps, but it's messy and there is a degree of randomness you can't avoid. (Yes you are right it's a terrible drawing. Promise you will forgive this when I'm giving you advice on presentation later!)

Also, you have other things going on (friends, family, health) which aren't always in your control, but you need to nourish and sustain.

Learn to Compartmentalise

Almost every person who reads this will be juggling one or more other roles as well as their work as a student: a part-time job, an internship, a search for jobs, moving between home and a new city which is going to be your workplace, parental or carer responsibilities, and other lives in terms of friends, hobbies, social media, sport, music etc.

You can feel pulled in different directions, almost literally.

Of course, these pressures apply much more so if you are doing your degree part-time. How do you juggle these roles?

Always keep in mind the main thing you must do is to finish.

This is your bottom line for the next few months. It sounds an obvious thing to say but this is crucial for people who have different roles to remember.

It's why I chose this title for the book.

Sadly, many people fail to finish. This means you need to have this very simple and brutal fact in mind.

You must finish. You will finish.

Imagine you have finished and rigorously work backwards to connect "now" to "the future".

Compartmentalise

To balance different roles: compartmentalise.

Things that help you compartmentalise:

- Please understand, on a very basic level, that multi-tasking is a myth. You do not have superpowers and like the rest of us you will only be able to do one thing at any one time.
- When you think you are multi-tasking you are switching between activities and doing all of them worse than if they were your sole focus.
- If you give yourself longer to do one thing, you will become more productive and efficient at it.
- You can recover the investment you make when you choose to spend a dedicated block of time on something. The way you recover this is by being able

to work better on that one thing than trying to do several things at once.
- Overall you save time - particularly if you also cut out wasteful activities. Resting and taking breaks are not wasteful, they are necessary.
- Carve out a regular block of unbroken time that is for your project.
- Make sure the block of time is long enough for you to switch gears from your other roles and commitments and make progress.
- If it is only 30 minutes, that may not be enough for you to build momentum. If it is longer than 90 minutes that is certainly too long for you to stay focused.
- It may take you 10 to 15 minutes to warm up. If you only worked in 15-minute bursts, and what is more this is flooded by pings and notifications you are wasting time. It is also bad for your brain.
- To be effective you need to focus. Give yourself a chance to do your best. You could even have shorter periods as long as the boundaries are there because this helps you focus – an approach called the Pomodoro technique is based on 25 minute bursts of working.

- Switch things off and work on one thing that will help you with your goal of finishing.
- Treat it like a job. Or, imagine you were paying someone else to do this. Think about how you would want them to work - then do that. That also involves resting by taking breaks and doing other things.
- Or, you could imagine you were starting your own business – something that required high-level concentration and sustained effort.

Show Yourself who is Boss

To juggle different roles, you can signal to your brain you are moving from working (or whatever else you want to spend time on) to studying.

Here are ways you can do this:

- Get changed into different clothes beforehand.
- Plan to work for a specific time on a specific thing.
- If you have a PC and a laptop use one just for studying while you are doing your project.
- If you don't have two machines, switch to a different background photo.

- On this different backdrop you could have a motivational saying or image you associate with success.
- If you can, work in a different physical space.
- If you must stay in the same space, change the lighting somehow, perhaps buy a lamp that you switch on and makes the desk space brighter and only use it for studying.
- Each time, before you start, say to yourself in front of a mirror "I am now going to work on my Dissertation" or "I am now going to work on my Thesis" depending on whichever term fits.
- You may feel silly doing it, but this works.
- You know those little pings and buzzes you think you can ignore – guess what: you can't! Every… single… ping… will distract you, break your flow, slow you down and waste your time.
- It could take you 15 minutes to get into the flow, then a ping means you start from scratch.
- Turn off your phone, log out of your Social Media accounts, close any tabs not to do with your studying. Take the battery out of your doorbell if you need to. Buy earplugs, whatever works.
- Do not have your email open on any device. I know I am repeating this, it is so important.

Remember the Project is an Opportunity

One thing that makes doing this hard is you may well be trying to do it alongside applying and looking for jobs. There is no denying there are pressures here.

But if you can, also think of this as an opportunity that can really boost your career. That will help you with your goals because that can help your motivation.

Often – and this is particularly true for Undergraduates – you will be an unknown quantity to potential employers.

If you can tell them a story about how your project really prepared you for the kinds of problems they are interested in, and how this has made you their ideal employee this could set you apart from other candidates.

There are several ways you could do this.

First, you could try to align – at least to some extent – the goals you have in your project and your career goals.

Choose a question and approach that you find interesting and will help.

Maybe you want to work in retail. If so studying the amazing success story that is Alibaba or the fall of some "bricks and mortar" chain-store could serve you really well. Or maybe you can show you can apply concepts from a history or even philosophy degree to (what employers would see as) the 'real world'.

Maybe if you are working in communications studies you can choose to look at how the shift to new forms of media is affecting traditional communication strategies and think what the implications for modern employers is.

Second, PLAN to think how you can use what you have learned about the topic.

It can be very helpful in a job interview to have in your mind several key facts and figures – how much market share a firm has, what happened to its share price over the last 5 years, what the major threat from competitors is, how it turned things around and so on.

These facts and figures sound impressive and you don't need to be doing business and management to know these.

This could be helped if you kept a diary during your project.

Third, as well as relevant knowledge about the topic, think about the kinds of questions you might be asked in a job interview.

Often interviews try to assess "behavioural competencies". So, they might try to find out if you could persuade people to do something by asking: "can you describe a time when you had to use your skills to influence someone."

You may be able to give examples of this in terms of gaining access – perhaps showing how you persuaded a company to trust you.

Fourth, and related to this, remember that you will be developing transferable skills you can talk about in an interview:

- Project management

- Time management
- Self-discipline
- Research skills
- Ability to focus
- Working independently
- Applying academic knowledge to real world problems
- In depth knowledge of a business problem

Fifth, remember it is worth thinking about how what you are doing could be described to different audiences.

Your project will often be of relevance to one or more of these areas that interest employers:

- Strategy (if you are doing anything to do with creating value or competition – also the context section of a setting will often include this)
- Human Resource Management (if you do anything relating to recruitment, pay, training, development, how people are managed – also if you interviewed people about their work experiences)
- Marketing and/or Sales (if you are dealing with a well-known brand or at some stage looking at how a

company promotes or sells its products or services, or communicates to customers)
- Leadership (if you apply this term loosely, as most people seem to, it's relevant to almost any setting)
- Change Management (if you were looking at how the company itself had changed, or how it was coping with an industry changing – and almost any industry is changing)
- Knowledge Work (this is true most obviously of technology companies or those working in IT or professional services, but often the way that companies in any sector create value is through some form of knowledge work)

Many, if not all these functions will feature if you even briefly interview someone about their own work environment.

For these reasons, even if collecting data is not a typical requirement, it can be a really good idea to do some interviews during your research.

What this will enable you to do is to tell a convincing and authentic story about what you learned about the above areas.

It will also help you to show in job interviews that you can communicate at a professional level.

Right! There is time for one more massive hack and then let's start to get more specific.

Start with the End in Mind

I've titled this section with a phrase associated with the writer Stephen Covey. His book *The 7 Habits of Highly Effective People* is great if you want to learn ways to work smarter.

As soon as you can, look at examples of completed projects kept by your institution (make sure they are in the same subject area, at the same level as the one you must do and follow the same requirements).

These should be accessible at your institution's library, or perhaps in an online repository.

If for whatever reason you cannot get access to these, you can look at online repositories at several institutions https://dash.harvard.edu/ is a good resource.

Ask your supervisor if you can see any completed projects they have supervised. They may not want you take one home – most likely because they will have loaned one out in the past and never got it back.

If you can anticipate this objection and assure them of its return they might let you have one.

Looking at other projects gives you an idea as to typical structure, what each section does and how many words there roughly are in each section.

I've done an example below, but you really won't get the benefit of this exercise unless you do this yourself.

This is partly because Universities have different requirements on word count - I'm just going to assume for the table below that your guideline length is 8,000 words.

Contents Page

Here is what your review could suggest a contents page would look like:

Section	Word Length	Purpose
Front matter		Satisfying university requirements e.g. declaration the work is your own

Acknowledgements	A paragraph, two at most	Thank friends/family, also typically a thanks to your supervisor
Abstract / Summary	150	See tips on "How to write an abstract"
Introduction	350	Sets out the topic says why it's important
Literature Review 1	1,000	Usually there are several strands to the review – don't write one lit. review chapter that is 3 or 4 times longer than any other chapter, structure chapters to be of approximately equal length
Literature Review 2	1,000	
Literature Review 3	1,000	
Context	800	Describes the place you focus on for your research and why it is a good setting to pursue your question
Method	500	How you carry out the research
Findings / Analysis	800	Reporting on what you found

Discussion	1,000	Discussing these findings in relation to the literature you reviewed
Conclusion	500	Summarising the study, explaining why your work was important
References	Any (not in word count)	Make sure this section is done properly and looks consistent and professional
Appendices	Any (not in word count)	Don't put anything important here – if it is important and you want it marked it should go in the text. Any supervisor will tell you appendices make no difference to your mark, but I suggest put something in just because it may look like you put more work in. It could be an interview schedule, a full version of the questionnaire, letters arranging access etc.

As you go through the process of writing, you can have a table like the one above that you update as you go along, with the number of words completed so far.

This will help you because it is a great way of keeping track of your progress.

It is also motivating because you can see how you will soon complete the first draft of some sections.

As mentioned before there is a need to have an eagle-eye view and doing a table like this can make sure you don't get lost in detail. Instead you will have the ability to make sure you are staying on target.

Get the Perfect Structure in 7 Steps

This section tells you everything you need to know about the abstract to a project and this is the key to great structure. An abstract is what you see at the beginning of every journal article. Length varies but it is often about 150 words long and is the first text that comes under the title.

Abstracts essentially tell readers what the paper is all about.

It may be a requirement for you to do one in your institution but even if it is not I recommend you have a section called "abstract" and that it follows the format suggested below. If your institution says it can be more than 150 – say 400, then follow that guidance and scale up from the example here.

It should be on a page of its own, under the header "Abstract". Don't call it summary.

In management, you could be asked to provide an executive summary. An executive summary is for people who won't have time to read the whole report – so it needs to be the first thing readers see. But you can always follow that with a page titled abstract.

Two advantages of setting out an "abstract" are:

(1) It will suggest you have been reading the right kind of academic work – journal articles.

(2) It should also signal you know what the expectations are of academic work and that you aspire to this.

But the biggest advantage is a little subtler than this.

The abstract is your golden opportunity to persuade the reader that you know what you have been doing, and to make the case that what you have done is a coherent piece of work that hangs together. Here we can usefully come back to the what and how distinction. The abstract will summarise WHAT your work is, but HOW you write the abstract really matters – it is the most important paragraph you will write.

A 7-step formula

Here is a way you can put an abstract together, using a 7-step formula (it needs to be in this order). I'm indebted to my friend Professor Stephen Brammer for teaching me a version of this.

You will be able to put a good case for what you have done if you can say:

1. what you are doing
2. why it is important
3. what is known
4. what isn't known
5. how you tried to find out what isn't known
6. what you found
7. why that matters

At UG and M-level you are not expected to do anything remarkably novel. There is not enough time. Indeed, you might not even have to do any data collection. Even so, and even if you are just doing an extended literature review, using this structure will make it sound like you have a well thought out argument. In fact it will also make you think more clearly about what you have done.

Here is a fictional example to help you. This is only 98 words so you can see how quickly you can use this 7-step formula:

> Amazon revolutionised retail, sparking a decline in bricks and mortar stores on our high streets. Though its rise has been meteoric, it is still not known whether there will always be a need for bricks and mortar stores for some goods. Interviews with 14 key stakeholders from industry, civil society and town planning suggest this picture is far from clear. Interestingly, in some cases, in what is an apparent paradox, increased "e-tailing" is associated with a parallel increase in the number of bricks and mortar stores. This suggests warnings about the death of the high street are premature.

Or, another way to show this would be:

Words from the abstract	Stage in the 7-step framework
Amazon	Step 1 – what you are doing
revolutionised retail	Step 2 – why it is important
sparking a decline in bricks and mortar stores on our high streets.	Step 3 – what is known
Though its rise has been meteoric, it is still not known whether there will always be a need for bricks and mortar stores for some goods.	Step 4 – what isn't known
Interviews with 14 key stakeholders from industry, civil society and town planning suggest this picture is far from clear.	Step 5 – how you tried to find out what isn't known
Interestingly, in some cases, in what is an apparent paradox, increased "e-tailing" is associated with a parallel increase in the number of bricks and mortar	Step 6 – what you found

stores.	
This suggests warnings about the death of the high street are premature.	Step 7 – why it matters

Part 2: Tips

"If we did all the things we are capable of, we would literally astound ourselves."

Thomas Edison

How to Do a Research Proposal

The requirements for a research proposal vary a lot across different institutions.

Here are some suggestions. These are quite in-depth because that is going to be of most help to you.

What a proposal should be able to do is to show your ability to:

1. Identify a reasonably clear problem or question
2. Break down that problem into a few Research Questions – that are well defined, interesting, feasible and so on (there's a section on Research Questions later)
3. Offer the beginnings of a review of the relevant literature – so that you can identify some influential theory/ies and give an impression of what is the current state of understanding
4. Describe the use of one or more potential research methods that are appropriate for answering the research questions
5. Identify any potential barriers or challenges to completing the research

6. Identify any ethical implications that arise from the proposed project

The core of this is 3 and 4: the review and the methods.

The Review

In the review you want to:

- Define key concepts (with appropriate citations)
- Identify central writers, articles, theories and frameworks
- Comment intelligently on the kinds of methods used in existing work
- Suggest gaps in understanding

Keep in mind that a literature review – done well – is NOT just reciting what other people have said. Try also to identify limitations in existing work.

The Methods

In the methods section you want to (not necessarily in this order):

- Explain the kind of data that you think is going to be required to address your research questions.

- You also want to justify your general approach (case study, qualitative, quantitative etc).
- You should also say something more detailed about your sample or interviewees: who they are, how they will be selected, how many there will be. Again, justify these decisions.
- Explain the methods in more detail and justify these.
- Maybe also say something about methodology – is your research taking a particular position like interpretivism or realism (terms that are explained later).

Mistakes to Avoid in Writing a Proposal

Be careful to ensure you do not just write a standard essay about a topic.

Be careful not to write a literature review that is based mainly on work on blogs and websites and doesn't obviously engage with the academic literature.

A similar mistake people sometimes make is to write a very general, abstract and almost philosophical kind of essay that is to do with research methods.

It is important to focus on the methods that are suitable for your project - but these are really secondary to what the existing academic literature tells us.

Remember, no methods are perfect, so you always need to show somewhere you are aware of the limitations of your project, of the kinds of data you are gathering, your proposed design and so on.

If you are struggling with thinking about methods, try to find a "footprint" article – an article where you can follow the methods used.

Related to this, don't miss out that there may be potential barriers to whatever design you use, or potential things that could delay your project.

How To Choose a Topic

One big reason people do not do well is through a poor choice of topic.

They can typically go wrong in one of two directions: making the topic too broad, or too narrow. If they do have problems then most of the time this will come from choosing something too broad. A consequence is their project lacks focus and it becomes difficult to answer the "so what" question – or, what is the contribution of their study.

The main ingredients in a topic are usually:

- A theory (from an article, author or book; often summarised in a model or framework)
- A problem (tax evasion, climate change, sexism)
- A context (a company, a sector, an industry or stakeholder, a function or practice)
- A method (interviews, surveys, documentary analysis, desk research)

Together these ingredients often make up the title too - you should really be able to tell a lot about the project from the title.

Let's illustrate this. Imagine someone wants to study Apple.

Now, you would know this is too broad because even though it's just one employer, well, the employer is Apple. I mean Apple, you know they're really big. Yuge.

You might be surprised how often a supervisor will ask someone what their idea is and get an answer back that is this broad.

When they do, inside, their heart sinks a little. Be more impressive than this.

Now let us imagine this person is more specifically interested in how Apple go about knowledge management.

It could be that they first working title they have, which captures their planned topic, is "Apple's approach to knowledge management".

Even though it's just one function (knowledge management) that's still way too broad in the timeframe you will likely have.

Focusing on a Topic

Here are 3 ways you can provide more focus to a topic that is too broad.

1. Be more selective and specific about the *theory*.

Perhaps you can do this by concentrating on what one or two key researchers have said about the topic area, or you can try to identify a key article, model or framework and use that to provide a frame of reference for the topic.

Using this example title about Apple, you could pick one perspective on knowledge management by someone called Ikujiro Nonaka.

One thing Nonaka does is differentiates between tacit and explicit knowledge (he didn't invent this distinction, but he made good use of it).

So, the more focused topic (and I will put it in the form of a title to help you also think about how these work) could be "Using Nonaka's tacit / explicit distinction to explain Apple's approach to knowledge management" – that's much better right?

2. Be more specific in terms of the *context*.

If you are looking at a large, multinational company, perhaps you can have more focus by concentrating on one element within the company, like its IT systems or corporate communications / intranet, or one function like sales or marketing, or maybe you can look at a layer of the hierarchy – middle managers or alternatively front-line workers.

Or you could look at a product line, or one kind of customer or the perspective of an investor or an industry regulator and so on.

So, the topic and revised title could be "Using Nonaka's tacit / explicit distinction to explain Apple's approach to knowledge management: an analysis of Apple's intranet"

3. You can also be more specific in terms of the *method*.

If you are collecting data you can choose to do interviews or surveys and once you think about where a logical place would be to get your sample from, this will help you narrow down.

If you are looking at secondary data sources, choosing to concentrate on one of these (annual reports for example) will also provide focus.

You need not necessarily specify the methods in the title but let's do this anyway.

So, a further revised title could be "Does Nonaka's tacit / explicit distinction help explain knowledge management at Apple: documentary analysis of third party descriptions of Apple's intranet".

This last version is very long, but it is still an improved topic because it is more interesting as a question, whereas the previous versions are statements. You would just need to be sure that you give an answer to this question.

Topic Choice and the Funnel

You might find this model helpful in thinking about how you get a more focused topic.

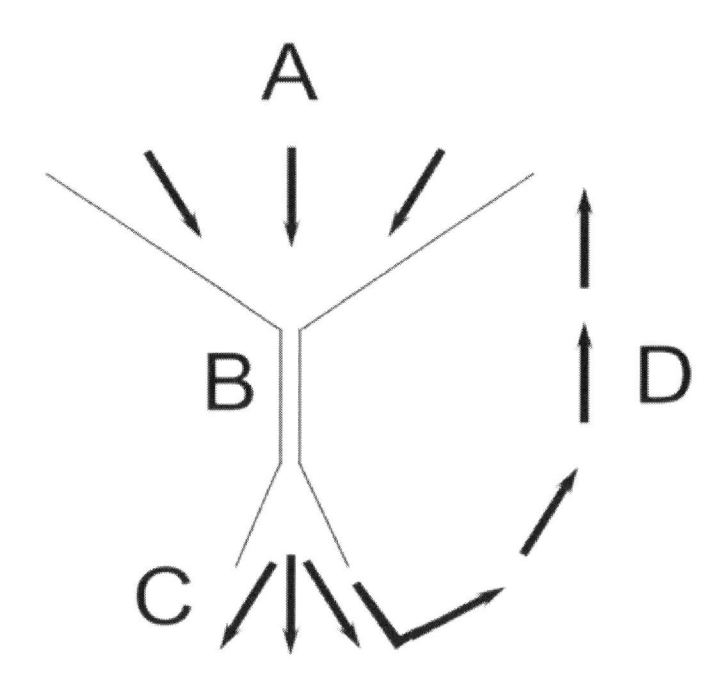

A – people start out with a very broad topic but ideally focus down using the steps suggested above

B – by the time they get to this stage they are focused - they have method, topic, theory, context defined, and these inform how they carry out the research

C – once they have their findings they broaden out (not as wide as they started out in stage A) because here is where they say what the implications of their study are

D – these implications feed back into the literature they initially reviewed showing how they support, or challenge some ideas - so they show they make a contribution to existing understanding

A note of caution here on stages C and D – keep in mind the requirements for UG and M-Level projects are not anywhere as high as for a PhD.

Choosing a Title

The Apple example above illustrates how to improve and refine the title. Another strategy you can use is two-part titles.

Two-part titles often have as the first part a general theme or topic area and in the second part a more specific application, problem or case.

One of my friends used to call this as "colon job" because a colon (:) often goes in the middle between these two parts.

Look out for it when you are doing your review. A lot of journal articles use this format.

Here are examples that connect a general body or bodies of literature to a more specific setting:

- Change management in a start-up: The case of Z-start
- Communication and identity: The dangers and opportunities of social media
- History and narrative: The fiction of "pure" historical texts

Here are examples of titles that connect a practice or method to a setting or problem:

- Getting customers hooked: The rise of incremental or "idle" games
- Ethnography, gender and time: Part-time work and the reshaping of motherhood

Here is an example where the general idea - relating to an emerging technology - is connected to a sector and company:

- How Blockchain changes everything: The case of financial technology at X-bank

Others could be answering a question:

- Corporate Culture or Corporate Cultures? The case of Y-retailer
- Is Maslow still relevant? The case of employee retention at …
- Post-Weinstein will we see permanent social change as usual? Gender dynamics at …

Let's drill down a bit into the title and topic by looking at Research Questions.

How To Choose Research Questions

These translate the overall topic into clear, researchable questions to guide your study.

It's better to have two or three Research Questions that you answer in depth than to have six or seven that you don't have enough time to go into in depth.

Here are examples of two Research Questions taking the above example – where we refined the topic and title of the project at Apple:

(1) Is Apple's intranet more accurately seen as a repository of explicit knowledge, or is it more accurately seen as the product of tacit knowledge?

This is good because it makes it clear what the theoretical concepts are, and it is the kind of question that would require some investigation.

Research Questions need to be clear, but they also shouldn't be too simple.

(2) To what extent is Apple's superior knowledge management about knowledge and to what extent is it about culture?

Again, that is a good Research Question because it asks an interesting question and it is one that invokes a theoretical concept or approach – the study of culture.

From this kind of question, you could imagine a programme of research – a literature review, appropriate methods and so on.

At the same time though "culture" is a huge subject. This means you would most likely need to explain what you meant but culture very soon after stating that question (if you did not say it in the question itself).

Your Research Question could be written as:

(3) To what extent is Apple's superior knowledge management about knowledge and to what extent is it about culture (i.e. "the way we do things around here")?

By putting this phrase in quotes, you are making it more specific and flagging up how it is you might understand and measure culture.

You might think about designing an interview schedule or topic guide in terms of those questions.

Just in case you see the phrase somewhere, another way to talk about what this phrase does, is that it "operationalises" the concept culture.

What are good Research Questions

Research Questions need to be symmetrical – whatever you find out in answer to the Research Question you need to be able to have a story to tell.

If you look at the first of these Research Questions above, it is symmetrical, it could be made into a non-symmetrical Research Question.

For example, it could have been written like this: is Apple's intranet the product of tacit knowledge?

That lends itself to a yes/no answer which you should avoid.

The first Research Question above has some similarities with yes/no but the phrase "more accurately seen as" implies there can be many outcomes.

Instead, if you ask is it more like A or more like B, it is easier to write about any outcome, either A, or B or (more likely) somewhere in between.

One useful phrase when writing a Research Question is "to what extent" – because this suggests a spectrum of outcomes.

Research Questions share the features of SMART goals – they need to be specific, measurable, achievable, relevant and time-bound.

In terms of the Achievable feature of SMART goals - Research Questions need to be feasible – you must be able to address them with the time and resources available.

If these questions above involved interviewing senior executives at Apple you would never gain access so that would not be feasible.

If your project involved a survey of Apple employees, the chances of a decent return would also be about zero.

However, looking at what data is already out there, provided there is enough out there, would be feasible.

An important aspect of feasibility is gaining access. It may sound harsh, but not everyone is going to be keen to spend time helping you collect data. They may simply not have the time.

Just think what you do when you get asked to participate in a short questionnaire when you are browsing on a website, or when you are asked to provide feedback on a service – how often do you take part?

Spend a fair bit of time thinking about your Research Questions, you are only going to have two or three so make them good ones.

Also – and this may sound obvious - try to get them right before you start trying to collect data.

Let's look at something now that, if it is done well, could make your project.

Get an 'Eagle-eye View' of Your Project

As mentioned in the previous section, my recommendation is that as soon as you can try to write an abstract (see 'get the perfect structure in 7 steps'). If you write a good one, this will summarize the whole of your document and give you a good "eagle-eye view".

When you are writing an abstract it doesn't mean you must stick with it for all time. What you should find is that you move back and forth from the detail of the text to this eagle-eye view. This means you will be periodically revising the abstract to make sure it is accurate.

It is another way to help you move between the WHAT and HOW. Let's show another way to think about the link between the abstract and your overall document.

This time we will add another column to the table introduced in the section - 'get the perfect structure in 7 steps'.

Words from the abstract	Stage in 7-step framework	Function

Amazon	Step 1 – what you are doing	Your Overall Topic
revolutionised retail	Step 2 – why it is important	Introduction
sparking a decline in bricks and mortar stores on our high streets.	Step 3 – what is known	Literature Review
Though its rise has been meteoric, it is still not known whether there will always be a need for bricks and mortar stores for some goods.	Step 4 – what isn't known	Ending to the Lit. Review the "gap(s)"; where you set out your research questions
Interviews with 14 key stakeholders from industry, civil society and town planning suggest this picture is far from clear.	Step 5 – how you tried to find out what isn't known	Your methods section
Interestingly, in some cases, in what is an apparent paradox, increased "e-tailing" is associated with a parallel increase in the number of bricks and mortar stores.	Step 6 – what you found	Your findings and analysis section, your discussion section too
This suggests warnings about the death of the high street are	Step 7 – why it matters	Your conclusion

premature.		

From this you can see how the abstract helps you think about the overall structure of your project.

It's also useful to look at some other things that can do this.

Referencing and Citing other Work

One thing that tends to set apart stronger work from weaker work is the number of references. This is a crude, not necessarily reliable measure, but you can almost guarantee your Supervisor will notice this.

They will also be marking several projects and this is one thing that is easy to compare or that they may compare subconsciously.

To state the obvious, it isn't just the quantity it's the quality of the work that you reference and how you use references.

Quality

In many subjects, you can think of a hierarchy of references:

Journal article > Book > Textbook > Magazine or periodical > Newspaper > Blog (by someone creditable) > Web page

This is very much a simplification. For example, in the Humanities (e.g. English, History) books are often still most prized.

Some journals are seen as better than others, some writers are seen as more prestigious, some book publishers are seen as better than others, some magazines or periodicals and Newspapers are seen as better than others.

These are matters of judgement. However, if your references section at the end is mainly made up of links to web pages, it will not look as well researched as someone who mainly refers to journal articles.

Why are Journal Articles Prized

Academic literature in journal articles is at the pinnacle of scientific knowledge. No other work is reviewed as rigorously or written as carefully as that produced by academics and their peers.

It can be challenging to read academic articles as they are written for an audience of researchers, but academic literature is still the best source of theory.

A theory is a structured and systematic attempt to explain things.

Theories do not just give us insight into individual events or contexts – this is what descriptions do.

Theories are more general and therefore much more useful because they allow us to try to explain what might happen in other settings, or even to predict what will happen in future.

The two key tasks in science are (1) to try to develop theory and (2) to test theory.

Often what people do is take a theory that has been used to try to explain something and then see how well that theory holds up in another setting.

An example might be taking a theory of networking that has been developed in studies in the U.S. and testing to see if it applies as well in China.

You might find there are similarities, but that the phenomenon of "guanxi" (https://www.investopedia.com/terms/g/guanxi.asp) is a different and important part of Chinese society and culture, and that this has a wider sense than "network" does. So the theory you tested is not a great explanation in this setting.

You might then try to develop the theory you tested to see if it can be improved.

If you read any academic article, you will find theories - attempts to explain something about the world - in many places.

One way to use academic literature is to find an article that outlines a theory relevant to your topic area, then test it to see how well that theory explains things.

How many References should I have?

People always ask me this, so I have stopped saying "it depends". For UG or M-Level aim for at least 60 references at least ½ from journals. For a PhD, aim for 250 references or more, with ¾ from journals.

There are no hard and fast rules and it is more important to read and draw on material intelligently.

If you are told to use a particular referencing style, use that from the beginning and throughout.

If you are not told, use Harvard referencing (rather than endnotes or footnotes).

"Harvard" means a citation to someone's work is made up of a name and a date and the citation goes in the text.

For instance, "Nor is there a single prescriptive route to developing an evidence base (Dopson, 2006)." The name is Dopson, the date 2006.

Again this varies across subject areas, work in the Humanities would often use footnotes extensively.

One common mistake people make is the opening half of their project has lots of citations, but in the later sections there are consecutive pages where no work is cited.

This is a very noticeable gap and easy to fix. Just don't have gaps like this!

Also make sure your Discussion chapter has a lot of references in it.

Ideally a lot of these will be the same ones that were in your review chapter.

This time though, when you cite these works, you will be commenting on them considering what you have found.

Remember, whatever method you choose (interviews, survey) will have a body of literature associated with it.

Look at the two paragraphs below (don't worry about the text itself):

Paragraph 1

> Discussion has centred on the practical, epistemological, or technical challenges prompted by an evidence based approach (Davies et al., 2000; Evans and Benefield, 2001; Nutley et al., 2003; Pawson, 2001). As yet, there are no definitively agreed criteria for what constitutes 'evidence' in management studies. Nor is there a single prescriptive route to developing an evidence base (Dopson, 2006). However, there is a growing body of literature and interest in this field (see also Craig, 2003; Denyer and Neely, 2004; Ellaway et al., 2001; Greenhalgh et al.,2003; Hewison, 2004; Leseure et al., 2004).

Paragraph 2

> Discussion has centred on the practical, epistemological, or technical challenges prompted by an evidence based approach. As yet, there are no definitively agreed criteria for what constitutes 'evidence' in management studies. Nor is there a single prescriptive route to developing an evidence base. However, there is a growing body of literature and interest in this field.

They are identical with one change. Paragraph 1 has references to other work, Paragraph 2 doesn't. Which looks more impressive? Do likewise.

Cite With Sophistication

A straightforward way of citing someone is to state an idea and put their name at the end of a sentence (like the example with Dopson just above).

But there are other, smarter ways to cite work.

For instance, if you want to explain that other people have more to say on a subject you can say "(see also Dopson, 2006)" or "(this argument is made more extensively in Dopson, 2006)" or you can say something more nuanced "(for a slightly different perspective that emphasizes the role of institutions, see Dopson, 2006)" or show there is controversy or disagreement "(someone who argues against this orthodoxy is Dopson, 2006)".

You can also use citations to show you have thought of other approaches but won't be pursuing them. For instance, "(it is beyond the scope of this project to discuss this in more depth, for a review see Dopson, 2006)." The approach taken here is predominantly at the micro-level, there are alternative perspectives at the firm or meso-level (Hewison, 2004), and at the national or macro-level (Dopson, 2006)"

These ways of citing work are more mature and sophisticated because they are more than simply slapping a citation(s) at the end of a sentence to show you know a relevant piece of work.

Instead, they try to position what you are doing much more carefully in relation to other work.

Similarly, look at these examples of progressively more sophisticated academic writing:

Progressively more sophisticated (same idea)	What's good/bad about this
Just description. Financial markets and the press often clung to Chairman Alan Greenspan's remarks. Because of the way he communicated, Greenspan was an effective leader of the Federal Reserve.	It comes across as descriptive or journalistic or impressionistic, some 'loaded' terms (leader, effective) aren't defined. What sounds like an explanation 'the way he communicated' is too vague to be considered theory.
Description + Citation. Financial markets and the press often clung to Chairman Alan	All that has been added is a citation but because that citation is appropriate (if you knew the source you would see this), it makes this seem

Greenspan's remarks (Bligh, 2007). Because of the way he communicated, Greenspan was an effective leader of the Federal Reserve.	less impressionistic, because it is reporting someone else's opinion.
Description + Theory + Citations. Smircich & Morgan (1982) argue leadership is "the management of meaning". This is a useful way to analyse Chairman Alan Greenspan's leadership because financial markets and the press often clung to his remarks (Bligh, 2007).	This is better again. There is an attempt to explain the phenomenon using an established theory – the rest of the article could go on to evaluate how well that theory (a general theory of leadership) worked to explain what was happening in that setting.

When do you use "et al."?

A convention if a work has 4 or more authors is to cite the first author and say et al. If you have 3 authors, the first time you cite a text you need to list all the authors' names, the next time just say the first author and then et al. (follow any guidance if you are given it).

So a citation to this article (as it would be listed in the references section): Brewster, C., Wood, G., & Brookes, M. (2008). Similarity, isomorphism or duality? Recent survey evidence on the human resource management policies of multinational corporations. *British Journal of Management, 19*(4), 320-342.

Would be to (Brewster, Wood and Brookes, 2008) first time and from then on (Brewster et al., 2008)

A citation to this book: (Wilkinson, A., Redman, T., Snape, E., & Marchington, M. (1998). *Managing with total quality management.* Macmillan: London.)

Would always be to (Wilkinson et al., 2008)

Also, et al. means "and others" - there is never an "and" before et al.

Don't plagiarise (use someone else's ideas or words without giving explicit credit)

If you take someone else's idea, give them credit for it. If you use someone else's words, put these in direct quotes and show where they come from.

Plagiarism is something supervisors hate. It is theft and it is a waste of our time to read something that has just been scraped from somewhere else.

Keep in mind that:

- Some people go out of their way to discover plagiarism
- It is easy to tell if the quality of writing varies substantially
- Supervisors won't want to give you the same credit as someone who has obviously worked by themselves
- You put a great deal at risk if you plagiarise work, including your degree and the classification of your degree
- Software for detecting plagiarism is improving all the time and the databases used are growing as more institutions share their data.

Sometimes people think it helps to get credit with someone else's idea or words.

The flaw with this perspective is it misses an important fact. In academic work you get credited when you identify something as someone else's idea and use it appropriately.

This is an important part of research and so there is no upside to plagiarising from that point of view.

A word of warning – be careful if you want to run your document through a plagiarism checker before handing it in. There might be a good, innocent reason for this – you just want to make extra sure that none of what you have written accidentally copies text from someone else.

The problem can be that some plagiarism checkers incorporate any text they check into their database. So, your work might later turn up as having a very high similarity score even if you had written it 100% by yourself (because it matches itself).

The safest thing to do is to just observe good practices. Make sure you always attribute an idea to its inventor and put any exact form of words you are taking from someone else in quotes and give the source.

Finding and Reading Articles

To get to the stage where you are referencing things you need to be able to:

1. Find relevant material
2. Read the material and make notes, including taking a note of the reference

Finding relevant material

To go into all the possible ways of searching for journal articles would need a separate book. Here are some quick tips to get you started.

Identify your topic, in terms of a two or three word phrase.

As an example, I will choose "product innovation" and concentrate in this section on business and management.

You will be able to see transferable lessons in your discipline.

Go to google scholar and choose advanced search

You will see an "exact phrase" box - put your two or three word phrase in this.

Tick the radio button for words occur "in the title of the article".

If you have identified the right phrase for your topic this search strategy should find papers where that is the main topic (because they use it in the title).

In the published in box type in speech marks "academy of management" so that this is the exact phrase Scholar will search for

×	Advanced search

Find articles	
with all of the words	
with the exact phrase	product innovation
with at least one of the words	
without the words	
where my words occur	● anywhere in the article
	○ in the title of the article
Return articles authored by	
	e.g., "PJ Hayes" or McCarthy
Return articles published in	"Academy of Management"
	e.g., J Biol Chem or Nature
Return articles dated between	
	e.g., 1996

©2017 Google LLC, used with permission. Google and the Google logo are registered trademarks of Google LLC

If you use the phrase "academy of management" Scholar will search for work in a much smaller subset of journals.

In this example it will find all the work meeting these search criteria that was published in the following journals:

- Academy of Management Review [theoretical, review papers]
- Academy of Management Journal [empirical papers]
- Academy of Management Perspectives [papers that are more for executives]
- Academy of Management Learning & Education [on teaching business and management]
- Academy of Management Annals [reviews the latest research]
- Academy of Management Discoveries [innovative approaches to research]

The Academy of Management is the peak professional body of academics in business and management.

The first 4 of these journals above are all extremely well regarded so this is a good strategy for quickly finding some of the best work in the field in this topic area. (There are some other journals that include the phrase "academy of management".)

If you find a paper with your topic in the title in any of these journals, this gives you a great basis for starting your literature review.

In particular, if you find a paper on your topic in the Academy of Management Review, that will refer to a great deal of relevant literature. That is because these are theoretical, purely conceptual, review papers.

You can also use the phrase "annual review" in the published in box. This now becomes more widely relevant to other subject areas.

If you do that, you will pick out another elite group of journals. Many are not going to be relevant but these could be:

- Annual Review of Economics
- Annual Review of Financial Economics
- Annual Review of Law and Social Science
- Annual Review of Linguistics
- Annual Review of Organizational Psychology and Organizational Behavior
- Annual Review of Political Science
- Annual Review of Psychology
- Annual Review of Public Health
- Annual Review of Sociology

Problems are often interdisciplinary – they might be partially answered with perspectives from economics, sociology, psychology, law, linguistics, politics even anthropology - or of course you might get very different perspectives which is itself interesting.

The advantage of doing this is you are then seeing how other disciplines might approach your same topic and you will be able to show a deeper appreciation of the topic area.

Sometimes if you hit on a key article it can unlock things for you and it can be the bedrock of your whole literature review.

In the published in box you can also put the key word for your discipline ("Sociology", "Geography" or "Communication" say) Scholar will search all journals which have that in the title.

Often, some of the longest standing journals in a given field will have the name of the discipline in.

How do you know if an article is "good"?

This is a very tricky question even for full-time academics to answer.

There are some things you can use as proxies (indirect measures) for article quality.

How many citations does it have in Google Scholar? If it has over 50 and is averaging 10 a year you could use that as a crude measure of quality. (This can differ massively across different disciplines, also newer articles haven't had a chance to clock up citations).

Where was it published? Journal quality is an even more divisive question (many of my European colleagues would be very cross the above only signposts you to North American and Annual Review journals for instance.)

There is some basis for evaluating how "good" a journal is in business and management, this is the Association of Business Schools list – the 2015 version is available on https://charteredabs.org/academic-journal-guide-2015/ (you have to register for the latest version).

This list is a subset of peer reviewed journals, ranked from 1 through to 4. A handful of 'world elite' journals that are 4*

A crude rule of thumb would be look out for papers in 3, 4 and 4* journals (again that would upset many of my colleagues).

You could also look at these:

- British Journal of Management (main journal of the British Acad. of Mgt. (BAM))
- Human Relations (very wide ranging, more critical papers)
- Journal of Business Ethics (good source of ethical issues in business and management)

- Journal of International Business Studies (international business)
- Journal of Management Studies (the leading non-US journal in management studies)

Remember: a good journal does not mean it is a good paper

If a journal has been going a long time that can sometimes be a sign of quality, but what is "a long time" does vary from discipline to discipline. Newer journals can be very good of course.

You can sometimes take a guess at this by looking at the reference to a journal.

Look at this article cited earlier: Brewster, C., Wood, G., & Brookes, M. (2008). Similarity, isomorphism or duality? Recent survey evidence on the human resource management policies of multinational corporations. *British Journal of Management*, *19*(4), 320-342.

The 19(4) part of this reference means that in 2008 this was the 19th volume (usually that will mean one volume a year) and the 4th issue of that volume (for a journal published quarterly there are 4 issues per year). So this journal was founded in 1990 – which in management is "a long time".

Finally, Wikipedia has a list of social science journals https://en.wikipedia.org/wiki/List_of_social_science_journals and because it only has a few journals per discipline many of these are longer established.

How to Use Google Scholar

Let me share with you one amazingly useful thing about Google Scholar.

Consider this: if you are reading a book or a journal article you can see other relevant work by looking at the list of references at the end.

This helps you look back in time - obviously the authors had to read what was in their references section before publishing their study.

What Google Scholar allows you to do is to track forward in time, which is useful if you think you have a bedrock article, but it is perhaps quite old.

To do this you just need to find the article and click on the "cited by" link to see where it has since been referred to in other work.

Google Scholar has another really great feature which will save you tons of time if you don't know about it already.

If you look at a source that has been identified (like the one below), underneath you will see the icon of a pair of quote marks next to the star (the star is a "save" feature).

Click on this and you will open a "Cite" box showing different ways to cite that article. You can then copy and paste whichever one you want (use the same one each time), and this will help you fill out your references.

(Scholar images are easier to view in the Kindle edition. Sorry if this is difficult for you and you are reading this in the paperback version. Print costs are as low as practical to keep the cost of the book down. If you follow the steps in the text it should make sense.)

Product innovation strategy and the performance of new technology ventures in China
MJ, K Atuahene-Gima - Academy of management Journal, 2001 - amj.aom.org
... legal, and financial institutions in **China** lead to environmental turbulence as well as dysfunctional competition (Nee, 1992; Peng & Heath, 1996; Xin & Pearce, 1996). We believe that the effectiveness of **Chinese** new technology ventures' use of a **product innovation** strategy may ...
☆ 99 Cited by 1311 Related articles All 9 versions
[PDF] researchgate.net

Strategic decision comprehensiveness and new product development outcomes in new technology ventures
K Atuahene-Gima, H Li - **Academy of Management** Journal, 2004 - amj.aom.org
... Compared with their counterparts in developed economies, new technology ventures in **China** face higher environmental uncertainty in terms of ... Together, these factors suggested that the **Chinese** new venture context offered a rich setting for examining the contingent effects of ...
☆ 99 Cited by 312 Related articles All 15 versions
[PDF] nchu.edu.tw

Absorptive capacity: A review, reconceptualization, and extension
SA Zahra, G George - Academy of management review, 2002 - amr.aom.org
... execution skills. These authors found that some firms possessed a strong ingenuity to understand complex technical problems but were not as effective in translating such knowledge into **product innovation** strategies. This corroborates ...
☆ 99 Cited by 9145 Related articles All 18 versions
[PDF] smu.edu.sg

©2018 Google LLC, used with permission. Google and the Google logo are registered trademarks of Google LLC

One last Google Scholar tip: in the image above, you can see links to the right-hand side say [pdf]. Often, though not always, this means you can access a free version of the article without having to log in through your institution's library.

Sometimes if that link is not shown and you click on the "All versions" link, that will expand to show (in the example shown) 9 versions of the article - one or more might be a free to access version.

This can save you time. It might not be the final version of the article though – the only meaningful difference there is the page numbers will not be accurate. The final version of a journal article will rarely start at page 1.

Reading articles

There is no getting away from it, reading journal articles is hard. More positively, it's a great way to build up your mental muscles and concentration.

There is a powerful hack here that can help you. For some people this can save them days if not weeks.

Keep in mind you don't need to read all sections of the article at the same pace or with the same level of effort. No academics do this.

Reading journal articles is not like reading your favourite piece of fiction where you want to take in every word.

You are – to some extent – reading instrumentally.

That is, when you read something you want to be sure that you get something from it that helps you, even if all that something is going to be is another paper that you cite in the text.

Here is one way to read a journal article:

Stage 1: Read the title – do you understand it and/or is it possibly relevant? IF NO keep searching for something else IF YES go to stage 2

Stage 2: Read the abstract (the short summary under the title) at least twice – do you understand it or at least most of it and/or is it possibly relevant? NO > keep searching YES go to stage 3

Stage 3: Read the paper focusing on the most important sections first. These are usually:

- The Introduction (sets context, outlines the main problem)
- The Discussion (sets out the contribution – that is what the paper has to say that is new, how has 'the literature' been moved forward)
- The Conclusion (summarises the paper)

If you understand these 3 sections and the abstract you know enough to write intelligently about the paper.

Some papers you are just going to use to drop in a citation to, others are going to be much more important. Spend your time on these appropriately.

Don't cite something you haven't read at least at some level, you could come badly unstuck and this brutally damages your credibility if it's noticed.

The hardest sections to read are usually the methodology and analysis sections, particularly with quantitative papers.

Don't try to follow the statistics in a quantitative study, but make sure you understand how the data was collected and what the data was.

Understand your Supervisor

One of the things about going through this process is there is a huge imbalance in power. And in case you were wondering, it's not in your favour.

This is true of many professions where you have an expert-apprentice relationship.

When you are doing a PhD, if it is going well, that is the kind of relationship you would expect to have.

But when you are at M-Level or UG Level you don't often have this kind of relationship.

Chances are your supervisor will have 5 or 6 other people they are supervising, and will be supervising (during the year) a mix of M-Level and Undergraduate students.

They will be juggling several projects and although they should give you great attention and focus when you need it, and although some institutions are better at putting the resources in to support supervision, the likelihood is you are not going to be as high on their radar as you might hope.

For these reasons, a phrase you might hear "managing your supervisor" can seem like a romantic ideal or naïve fantasy. But here is an important idea that will help you: it's even more important to try to do this kind of thing well when you have less power.

Managing your supervisor involves setting their expectations, creating an impression of yourself which is helpful to you, and trying to influence them – ethically - so that their decisions positively benefit you. It is what we learn to do in professional relationships.

Basically, given your limited power and their limited time, you are trying to get the best from them, for your interests.

Empathise with, and "Manage" your Supervisor

There is a great deal of variety in what academic work involves, and it's also tremendously rewarding. The popular stereotype of someone resting in an ivory tower, with lots of time on their hands, is way off the mark though.

Higher Education has changed remarkably in the last 15 years or so. There are a lot of pressures – to satisfy rising expectations among students, to publish, to do well against various performance criteria and metrics.

These are taking place against a backdrop of the erosion of working conditions, cuts to pensions and increasing precariousness. You need to get the most you can from whatever time and support you get from your supervisor.

Take a minute to imagine you are a full-time academic. This exercise will enable you to empathize with your supervisor and this will help you manage more effectively. To help, here is a sketch of what a lot of academics might be having to cope with.

- You might be supervising projects from maybe 6 M-Level, 12 UG and 4 PhD students.
- On top of these things you could teach 4 courses a year, one at least could be a large course of over 100 students, each of whom can ask you at any time for help.
- You must do the marking for these courses and mark the resits, so you need to set two exams if that is the format.
- If the assessed work involves assignments you need not just to mark these but provide feedback which is detailed and specific at the same time as not leading to complaints or accusations you have not marked consistently.
- You will most likely have to deal with some complaints and accusations in any case, the best you hope for is you have fewer of them. As well as your course you will need to be a second marker on several other courses.
- As well as the students you supervise and teach, you might have 20 UG personal tutees, 5 M-Level personal tutees. For your tutees, you are expected to give advice to each of them and write references for each of them. You will get a lot of reference requests, some from people who graduated years ago.

- On top of that, in many institutions you are expected to publish, go to conferences, bring in grants, and create an impact with your research. This can cause a lot of pressure and stress.
- To do this you need to keep up to date with the literature – of which there is too much to read even if you were doing nothing else. You also must put yourself through the horrors and rollercoaster ride that is peer review.
- If you are trying to publish you will need to referee for journals which is one of a lot of unpaid "pro bono" activities. If you are not expected to publish then you can perhaps double the teaching commitments above.
- You will also most likely have an administrative role, maybe you are Director of a programme or an Admissions Tutor or you are associated with a Research Group.
- You will be in several professional networks and occasionally might get asked to comment by your media office or field calls from a very broad range of stakeholders. You will get a lot of these so there is not time to deal with each in detail. You will get a ton of email and a ridiculous amount of spam.

The point of writing all this is that supervisors don't mind being "managed" by supervisees because of the variety and amount of work they must get through. (Although – personally I would not use this exact phrase.)

If you are "managing" them by working to build up an authentic impression of being professional and organised from the very first meeting, inside they will feel relief and gratitude.

The relief and gratitude they will have is because they will hope you are not going to be very difficult to work with and to try to help. After all, they have to manage you.

Meeting Your Supervisor

If you have a meeting with your supervisor, remember that they will have a very long to-do list of other things.

If you are one of their supervisees here is how you set yourself apart from others:

- Turn up prepared, and look prepared

- Read the relevant guidance on assessment, perhaps in a module guide or handbook
- Create the impression you are organised
- Plan beforehand what you want to get from the meeting, but also be flexible
- Carry a decent quality notepad
- Have a list of things you want to cover or learn more about in a meeting (be careful what is written on that list – because they may ask to see it to save time)
- Try to read something they have written
- Show you respect and value their time
- Be not just ready to work but show you have already done some work
- If they have asked you to do something, be sure you did it - and a little bit extra - and be enthusiastic about it "I found that really helpful" "thank you I found that interesting"
- Dress smartly (sorry, it shouldn't matter, but it can do)
- Smile (sorry, it shouldn't matter, but it can do)
- Have some clear ideas but be ready to listen and to change direction with advice
- Be one of those supervisees who reads what they are asked to

- Be someone who is on a personal level – enthusiastic, friendly, professional, considerate
- Don't interrupt
- Be careful of one thing – when your work is in its later stages is going to be something you are very close to, this can mean you take criticisms personally
- Do not rush to defend yourself against criticism
- Every criticism is your friend
- Every criticism represents a golden opportunity for you to show that you have listened to advice and improved… to say things like "oh yes", "oh I hadn't thought of that", "that's a good point", "I shall have to think about that, thank you" then in the next version show you have listened. This isn't a way of 'faking it' with your supervisor, it will help you to stay sincere and authentic and if you act consistently with your words it will improve your work and your prospects.

Questions Not to ask and what Not to Say

- How often do we need to meet?
- What is the best way to contact you?

- How long will it take you to read something I've written?
- How many hours a week should I be working?
- Supervisors like talking about ideas, they don't like talking about process - deadlines, extensions, formatting requirements, word count. So…
- Don't waste time by asking anything that is answered in your institution's guide or handbook (which has a lot of information)
- If you are unfortunate in having medical problems, or illness in the family or that affects pets, do not give graphic or detailed descriptions of these problems.
- If these mean you may want to ask for an extension then you would need to provide sufficient detail and a suggestion would be do not elaborate unless needed.
- It's a professional relationship. If you are even able to say that you would prefer to keep the relationship focused on work that will win respect.

Good questions to ask your Supervisor

"I would like to make as much progress independently as I can, could I get some feedback from you after the first draft of the review and methods chapters [if you are collecting data] or would you recommend my sharing something with you before then?"

Why this is a good question: it signals you are not constantly going to be seeking help and asking questions at every stage; it shows you can plan ahead and shows discipline; it shows you understand that a critical phase in a project is to have feedback before you collect data; if (in your view) you are getting less support than you need then you can either try to press for this – which may not be the best tactic, or try to reframe this as you are working independently; then use the phrase "working independently" into conversations you have with your supervisor.

"Are there any articles in particular that you would recommend me reading in this area or should I just use my judgement?"

Why this is a good question: it shows you are willing to use your judgement and expecting to do so. A slightly subtler reason is that it gives you an insight into any favourite approaches your supervisor might have and it also gives them a face-saving "way out" if they are not an expert in the area you are studying.

"I read your paper in [some journal] and was interested by the idea of [x] or the method you used of [y]. Do you think I might be able to link this somehow to the topic which interests me which is [z]?"

Why this is a good question: your supervisor will be surprised and pleased that a student has read their work and she will be immediately more interested in your project. Make sure you understand what they have written because they will read any description of their work closely.

Don't use creepy phrases like "internationally renowned" or whatever to describe them or their work if you do cite them.

Some Advice on Research Methods

There isn't scope in this book to say very much that is technical about methods or about more philosophical and technical questions to do with epistemology and ontology.

These are quite thin notes or perhaps things that might help you remember what you hopefully covered in lectures.

But it is helpful even so to recap some of these ideas because they can take time to sink in.

Here is a list of possible methods

- Survey (closed item, open item, mix)
- Interviews (open-ended, semi-structured, structured, critical incident)
- Focus-groups (open-ended, semi-structured, structured, critical incident)
- Observation (time and motion study, non-participant, participant, covert, ethnographic, anthropological)

Case study (case study is a research design that usually incorporates multiple methods, so it could include any of the above)
- 'Discourse' analysis (this phrase is often loosely used, essentially a basic idea in Discourse is that language shapes the social world, it does not just describe it)
- Narrative analysis (the focus is more on story-telling and on how someone's account of a phenomenon is put together rather than focusing on what they say)
- Documentary analysis (there are several approaches to analysing documents - data sources could include corporate documents, websites, intranets, minutes of meetings, policies and procedures, manuals, advertisements, features in the press or periodicals and magazines)

For help with Interviews try: https://www2.open.ac.uk/students/skillsforstudy/conducting-an-interview.php

For help with Surveys try: https://socialresearchmethods.net/kb/survey.php

Which method you choose depends on:

- Research Questions
- The Kind of Data You want
- The Kind of Data that You can get
- Your Beliefs and Values
- Ethics
- Goals
- Your Skills (and your willingness & time to develop new ones)
- Feasibility (time, costs, access)

Terms to do with the Philosophy of Research

Very briefly, some of the terms you might want to know, or use are:

Epistemology: to do with the nature of knowledge

This is quite an important term that people don't always understand but it is not difficult. To help understand it, here is a list of "epistemological" questions:

What is knowledge?	How do you know?
Who can know?	Why should I believe you?
What kinds of things can be	

known?	Can you prove it?
How can they be known?	What evidence do you have for that?

In this table on the left-hand column are the more abstract, philosophical questions. In the right-hand column are questions you can keep at the back of mind when reviewing other work.

For a convincing project, you need good answers to these questions to come through in your own work.

Ontology: to do with the nature of being – beliefs about what things exist.

For instance, imagine that you think only people can be held responsible as ethical beings. If so, then it would not exactly be accurate to say "Tobacco company X is guilty of killing people". The question would be about which individuals are responsible. This could have important implications – for instance rather than fining a company you might prosecute the Chair or CEO.

Positivism: This is a belief system or approach about how the social world can be studied and it involves some epistemological and ontological assumptions.

Positivism holds that the social world exists independently of our minds or perceptions i.e., there is a real world out there (this belief links positivism to the label realism, but positivism is a pejorative or derogatory label).

Also, positivists believe that: there are some social facts that exist and speak for themselves and so do not require interpretation; that researchers can discover facts by using the right methods and techniques; that knowledge progresses incrementally as we discover new facts and corroborate or falsify then improve on existing theories; furthermore, when they discover the facts they believe they can establish laws that can predict and control the social world.

Interpretivism: Interpretivists believe that the natural world and the social world are different – human beings are thinking subjects who give meaning to the social world and bring that world into being when they give it meaning and when they talk about it.

They believe there are no social facts free of interpretation and that researchers should understand how people and communities construct their social world by giving it meaning (a related term for this position being constructivism).

Whether something social is seen as true is held to be culturally and situationally specific.

Interpretivism is very often held out as the opposite of positivism. Saying opposite is a simplification though because there are a great many different positions one could take on these questions. Any two different positions would not be different in terms of just one dimension.

Key Mistake to Avoid

The most common mistake students make in relation to these issues is to describe themselves somewhere as interpretivist but then somewhere else they go on to talk about their data and context in a realist way.

Really, you don't need to make grand statements such as "I am adopting an interpretivist perspective" or "I am a realist".

People tend to write about these things in a more sophisticated way – for instance, saying "To try and gain access to the way these interviewees understood their organizational culture, I asked them whether there were any things that could be seen as sacred or forbidden".

You could then say, "This is consistent with an interpretivist tradition".

Methods: techniques, procedures and perhaps instruments for collecting data as well as analysis.

Methodology: the study of methods (asking whether a certain method would *really* answer a research question is not a question about method, it is about methodology).

Some people say these terms mean the same thing and some people use them interchangeably. They are different, but they also overlap.

For example, if you choose this method: large scale, closed item remotely administered questionnaire… that is on the realist end of things, so it involves methodological commitments.

Qualitative: data that is in the form of talk or texts, or symbols, including observational data.

Quantitative: data in numerical form or that can be reduced to or represented by numbers.

Quantitative data tends to be associated with realist assumptions. But be careful because although in research qualitative data is closer to interpretivism, some qualitative data is also realist – such as some uses of structured interviews in market research.

Validity: can refer (speaking simply) to Internal validity – questions about the robustness of the design and methods – did they measure what they were supposed to; or to External validity - the likelihood that patterns observed are present in the wider population i.e., statistical or empirical generalizability

Reliability: this involves asking about the extent to which we can expect findings to be replicated if the study was done with the same participants in the same context

Objectivity: this involves asking whether we can be sure that the findings are reflective of the setting and the subjects and the pursuit of the research questions, rather than being the product of the researcher's own biased thinking?

These last three criteria are mainly used to evaluate quantitative research.

Qualitative research is harder to evaluate in some ways, but the main questions are to do with plausibility and with evaluations as to whether the researcher has shown they are critically reflexive.

Whether the findings apply in other settings is still an important question of generalizability, but this is not based on statistical inferences.

Part 3: Writing Tips

"You will find the key to success under the alarm clock."

Benjamin Franklin

How to Start

Starting to write something is hard and a lot of writing involves revising what you have written but the key thing is to get any thoughts out of your head and onto a page.

Writers through history have had a fear of a blank page, but modern technology can be helpful - there are 3 main ways you can try to get what's in your head onto a page:

(1) Write the old-fashioned way with pen and paper first
(2) Type it up on your PC or laptop
(3) Dictate using a voice recognition programme or the notes function on your phone. The great thing about dictating is you can do it anywhere.

Set yourself a goal of writing at least 150 words before you stop to review and think about what you have written. You may find it helpful just to jot down bullet points.

Here is a really unusual tip that might help you if you are stuck. If you can't think what to write, flick through a dictionary and choose a noun at random. Then, make yourself write a sentence that uses that noun relating it to your Dissertation. This will force you to think in a different way and also – in a slightly odd way – to focus. Once you have written that sentence see if you can keep going and after a while you can revise the work. It can be much easier to revise a page that has a lot of shortcomings than it is to write something from scratch based on a blank page.

How writing works

If it is reasonably well structured, your work should be made of: sentences, paragraphs, sub-sections (a group of paragraphs under a sub-header) and sections (chapters).

- A sentence expresses one main, complete idea or thought.
- A paragraph groups several connected sentences together.
- A sub-section organises related paragraphs together.
- A section, or chapter, includes these sub-sections in a logical order.

The most important sentence in any paragraph is the first sentence. Always make sure this is clear and well written.

The most important paragraph of any chapter is the first paragraph. Always make sure this is clear and well written.

The most important paragraph is the abstract. Keep going back to this to make sure it is clear. It will change as your project progresses.

- Don't have sentences that are too long (there is a section on this below).
- Don't have paragraphs longer than a page.
- Have sub-sections of approximately equal length.
- If you want to make life simple for yourself then only use 3 levels of text: Chapter headers, Sub-section headers, and normal.
- Use the Styles feature in WORD to categorise this text.
- For the Chapter Headers use the style Heading 1
- For the Sub-section headers use the style Heading 2
- If you are using WORD, you can then easily generate a Table of Contents (go to references, insert table of

contents, custom contents then choose 2 levels of heading). This route may differ depending on what version of WORD you use.

"Signposting" to help the Reader

This will be a long document, you want to make it easy to read.

You can think about this as signposting - sometimes people also talk about creating a trail of breadcrumbs to follow.

Start each chapter with an introduction, end each chapter with a conclusion.

In the introduction of a chapter, say what you will do in the chapter and explain how this follows from the last chapter.

In the conclusion of a chapter, recap what you have said in the chapter and then explain what will be in the following chapter.

Even if you do nothing else, this will improve the sense that your work is well structured.

Use lists and bullet points

If your work is just a series of paragraphs of text without any lists or bullet points it will be harder to read.

You don't want to overuse them but lists and bullets are a good way to summarise and organise your thoughts, or to review what others have said.

Lists and bullet points can also be rhetorically effective because – at least in visual terms - they can create a sense that you are organised and in command of a topic.

They can also convey that you have done more work that is underlying the list.

Of course, this impression depends on your having created a list that is sensible and that doesn't have obvious omissions.

Understanding Sentence Structure

There are a few grammatical errors that are quite common to different people. Without getting too technical there are some quick hacks you can do to improve your grammar and readability.

Don't have overly long sentences

How long is too long? A suggestion would be not to have any sentences longer than 30 words.

If you do have sentences that are longer than this, just break them up into two or more. Here's an example:

> Amazon clearly faces a problem in terms of good corporate citizenship - because it has to solve how to trade off the challenge of pursuing corporate social responsibility against a seemingly unstoppable rise in demand for its products, when demand growth can only be met in some situations in the future by continuing to rely on traditional delivery methods, meaning they are likely to increase their carbon footprint.

This reads badly, it could be two sentences:

> Amazon clearly faces a problem in terms of good corporate citizenship because it has to trade off the challenge of pursuing corporate social responsibility against a seemingly unstoppable rise in demand for its products. Demand growth can only be met in some situations in the future by continuing to rely on traditional delivery methods, meaning they are likely to increase their carbon footprint.

Or three sentences:

> Amazon clearly faces a problem in terms of good corporate citizenship. This is because it has to trade off the challenge of pursuing corporate social responsibility against a seemingly unstoppable rise in demand for its products. Demand growth can only be met in some situations in the future by continuing to rely on traditional delivery methods, meaning they are likely to increase their carbon footprint.

Or four sentences:

> Amazon clearly faces a problem in terms of good corporate citizenship. This is because it has to trade off the challenge of pursuing corporate social responsibility against a seemingly unstoppable rise in demand for its products. Demand growth

can only be met in some situations in the future by continuing to rely on traditional delivery methods. This will mean they are likely to increase their carbon footprint.

Which do think is best?

If you write in shorter sentences this will make you write more clearly and it will also make you think more clearly.

Having this kind of clarity is especially important for the very beginning, and it also matters for the introduction, the statement of research questions, the contribution, and for the beginning and final paragraphs of each chapter.

As well as clarity, let's think about how to give you writing more impact.

There are 7 main different parts of speech: nouns, verbs, adverbs, adjectives, prepositions, conjunctions, pronouns (and interjections which are more typical in speech).

The table below shows these with examples taken from the extract above.

Parts of Speech Made Simple

Part of speech	Role in a sentence	Examples
Nouns	Naming words	Amazon, problem, citizenship, demand, products
Adjectives	Describe nouns	Good, unstoppable, traditional
Pronouns	Stand in place of nouns	It, they, their
Verbs	Action words	Faces, is, met, increase, rely
Adverbs	Describe verbs	Clearly, seemingly
Prepositions	Show relationships between words	Against
Conjunctions	Joins words or phrases together	Because

Now let's look at tense: in other words, the time something happens, has happened, or will happen.

You won't realise it when you speak your first language, but tense is very complicated.

To make it simpler we will look at three broad times you might write about (present, past, future) and another tense which is about things that could happen - the conditional tense (sometimes called the subjunctive).

Tenses Made Simple

Tense	Example
Present	Amazon face (a problem); is facing; has been facing
Past	Amazon faced; was facing; has faced; had faced; had been facing
Future	Amazon will face; is going to face; will be facing; will have faced; will have been facing
Conditional	Amazon could face; could be facing; could have faced; could have been facing

These two tables are useful to consider together because they help to think about how to give your writing more impact.

Nouns are how we think about categories and definitions. You need to have a clear idea about the main nouns you use, and to be clear how you define them and about what categories they belong to.

Using the example above, do you understand Amazon primarily as: A Multinational Company, a digital giant, a good investment, a very large employer, a logistics company, a unique success story, an example of successful strategy, a company that causes pollution, a company that should pay more tax or some combination of these?

The action words in a sentence are the verbs, the most impactful tense for verbs is the present tense and verbs are also most impactful if it is the main noun in a sentence that has carried out the action of the verb.

If the main noun carries out the action of the verb, these verbs are called active verbs, and this is the active voice - for instance, "Amazon faces a problem".

In the passive voice, the main noun in a sentence is acted on by the verb - for instance, "a problem is faced by Amazon".

To make an impact, whenever you can, write in the present tense. Also, choose your verbs well to make them interesting and to have variety. Also, make them active verbs.

Using the example again of Amazon facing a problem you could choose any of the following words or phrases instead of "face": confront, struggle with, try to resolve, cope, reconcile, wrestle with, grapple with, is preoccupied by, tackle, must challenge, must oppose, must address, must resist and many others.

Why Verbs beat Nouns

Another thing to keep in mind is that verbs are very often the things that grab our attention in sentences.

You might think that choosing the right nouns and adjectives is what gives your work colour or makes it impactful, but it is the verbs and adverbs you choose that make most impact on the reader.

Verbs, and less so adverbs, tell us something dynamic about how things are related or what is happening, or will happen.

Nouns can be a bit static or even lifeless, verbs bring ideas to life and give sentences their impact.

You could try this. It may or may not help you.

For your project, spend five minutes in total thinking about each of these things:

1. the main nouns
2. how you define these nouns and what categories you see these nouns as members of
3. the main verbs – the ways that these nouns act (remembering to choose verbs carefully to make these clear, accurate, impactful)
4. more exciting and dramatic verbs.

You may well be surprised how much clarity this simple exercise can give you in terms of getting straight in your head what you are trying to say on paper.

It can help you keep your eye on the big picture. If you find it helpful, do it again once you are further progressed.

What this can help you think about is what is sometimes called the contribution. Usually the findings will be something you can explain in terms of a key noun and a key verb.

To talk about the wider implications or contribution it will often be whether you can say something new about the category that your key noun belongs to.

Let's take the example of Amazon facing a problem relating to its carbon footprint and Corporate Social Responsibility (CSR).

There are 3 nouns in this phrase: Amazon, the problem of its carbon footprint (I'm counting that as one noun), and CSR.

Let us say you examined this by talking to some regular customers of Amazon – that is another noun.

Your main story is going to be something that can be summarised in one sentence that connects two or more of these nouns with a main verb.

You should be able to explain the essence of your Dissertation by showing how a verb acts on one or more of these nouns, and then you should be able to say something about the broader implications by expanding out from this to say what that says about the broader category.

For instance:

> Amazon can only face this problem in future if it: innovates / improves marketing / passes on costs to customers

/ educates customers / absorbs costs. The implications are that MNCs / online retailers / digital giants need to innovate / improve marketing etc.

Amazon operates online but still must face the problem of having a carbon footprint. The implications are that even online retailers / digital giants cannot escape their footprint.

Amazon customers don't connect their purchase behaviour with Amazon having a carbon footprint. The implications are that where customers use online retailers they may need educating / incentivising / nudging.

Don't Split Infinitives

If you just read that and thought "what?" don't worry, you are not alone. So, what is a split infinitive? The infinitive just means a verb in its simplest form, with "to" in front: to read, to move, to hear, to see are all infinitives.

A split infinitive is where you have a word in between the "to" and the verb form: to swiftly read, to silently move, to barely hear, to clearly see are all split infinitives.

The most famous split infinitive is from Star Trek "To boldly go…" (incidentally this sounds a lot better than "to go boldly").

The reason they are not liked by some is because in Latin verbs that are in the infinitive form are only one word. In Latin, to read is *legere*, to move is *movere*, to hear is *audire*, to see is *videre*, so it wouldn't be possible to put another word "in between".

Here are split infinitives plus fixes:

- We have to immediately decide > We have to decide immediately
- My advice is to not use that > My advice is don't use that
- You need to quickly read this > You need to read this quickly or you need to speed-read this

Most people don't know what split infinitive means. Maybe your supervisor doesn't know either.

But my suggestion is you should avoid them because either they might know or, even if they don't know explicitly, it could unconsciously affect how they evaluate your writing.

Some people are delighted that they know what a split infinitive means. They feel clever for knowing this and enjoy "correcting" them. In their minds, they have found something wrong.

Other people will tell you a split infinitive isn't an error and that it's just convention. I agree but the simple fact is some people don't like them and no-one notices when you don't.

Subject verb agreement

This is another rule people might not necessarily be able to define, but they will be able to see it as an error in your work if you don't follow it.

For the subject and verb to "agree" they need to be matched in terms of number and person.

If you have a singular subject and use the singular form of a verb or you have a plural subject and use the plural form of a verb that is agreement in terms of number.

If you are using the 1st person (I), 2nd person (you), or 3rd person (he, she, it, they) for the subject, then the verb also needs to be the same.

This all sounds simple, but it can get tricky with longer sentences and harder to see as a mistake by the writer.

For instance: "In relation to creativity and wealth, the real and lasting contribution of motivational speakers - like Les Brown, Zig Ziglar, Tony Robbins and Jim Rohn, are to trigger abundance in both."

In terms of number the subject is singular ("the... contribution") and when reading this sentence, it might have jarred slightly that the verb was plural ("are").

But this mistake is very easy to make as a writer and can be hard to spot in one's own work. I've probably done it in this book at least once.

One suggestion is simply to be aware of this problem. Another is to keep in mind there could be several nouns between the subject and the verb. Another is to write shorter sentences and to aim for clarity.

Should you Use "I" when Writing

A common question that students have is can they, or should they, use the word "I" to describe the choices they make and their interpretations and analysis.

Technically, this is a question about "voice" and whether you should write in the 1st person or the 3rd person.

1st or 3rd Person

In the 1st person you might say, "I interviewed six regular users of Amazon to see whether…"

In the 3rd person this is, "Six regular users of Amazon were interviewed to see whether…"

If you are following the advice about using active verbs, and writing in the present tense, then you would prefer to use the 1st person.

Also, at least I would say, with some kinds of research – like interviews - it makes more sense to use the 1st person because it is clearer that what follows is your interpretation. You are acknowledging your role in the research process.

Sometimes this choice is a matter of personal style though and my advice is you want to be pragmatic and to write in the style your supervisor is used to or prefers.

You might just find you have a supervisor who prefers that you use the passive voice – perhaps they have been taught themselves it sounds more scientific, maybe they come from a particular research tradition.

How do you know? The simplest way to check this is to ask your supervisor. "Would you advise that I use "I" when talking about my research or is it better to use the passive voice". Don't make this the first question – it's not that big a deal.

If your supervisor doesn't know what passive voice means you can use the example above. Do this at the beginning because otherwise it could be a pain to change it at the end.

Listen carefully to their answer, most supervisors I know would not want to be too prescriptive – we don't tend to like giving rules to our supervisees because we want them to find their own way.

It may be that they say you should use whichever you prefer, but if you listen closely you will most likely be able to detect a personal preference – go with that.

If they say they are fine with or even prefer the first person that is good because you can use active verbs and the present tense, but even so still don't over-use "I".

Even if they tell you that they are fine with 1st person, if you overuse "I" you will create, almost on a subconscious level, an impression your work is too subjective or impressionistic.

Avoiding 1st or 3rd Person

Now here is some good news. With a little effort you can describe your research in such a way that you do not use either 1st person or passive voice.

Here are some examples, first in relation to interview research:

"Six regular users of Amazon were interviewed to see whether…" (passive voice)

Or

"I interviewed six regular users of Amazon to see whether…" (active voice)

Can be written as:

"The interviewees are shown in Table 1. The following extracts from the interviews indicate that…"

(quick tip: words like "indicate", "suggest" and "seem / appear" are usually more appropriate in the social sciences than "demonstrate", "show" … don't use "fact" and "prove" unless you feel very brave).

Similarly, take this (passive voice) example of describing a survey:

"The survey was sent to an initial sample frame of 220 employees which yielded 76 usable, complete surveys. This was a response rate of 34.5%"

"Table 1 shows the initial sample frame of 220 employees, yielding 76 usable, complete surveys. This represents a response rate of 34.5%"

Both these examples give you a quick hack for being able to talk in the present sense.

If you put up a diagram showing what happened (which is the past tense), you can talk about what the diagram shows (using the present tense).

Vocabulary Building - Describing Relationships

Often when we do academic research we are trying to relate two nouns to each other in some way: for instance a demographic variable and an outcome like income; or a firm's growth and performance; quality and return on investment; training and employee turnover; reputation and carbon footprint and so on.

Or, you might be looking at how to relate one or two ideas that connect to a phenomenon (or thing) – a broader problem or topic of interest. For instance, how does the idea of network capital help understand - gang activities, or the environment of Orange County, or a social practice such as initiation rituals, or symbols and markers like tattoos, gang signs and emblems.

Very often you will find it helpful to focus your ideas and that might well mean you end up looking at two main nouns, let's call them "A" and "B".

There are dozens and dozens of ways of talking about the relationship between two nouns and aiming to do this in a sophisticated way is a good thing.

Here are some of the ways you can talk about how one noun "A" relates to another "B".

No relationship - no evidence of a relationship / no discernible relationship / apparent absence of a relationship / no basis to infer a relationship with these data / in these interviewees there was little to suggest a relationship

Correlated positively or negatively - no apparent evidence of correlation / some evidence of correlation / weak correlation / a larger sample or more evidence would be needed to establish whether this were genuine correlation / although this is visually indicative of or suggestive of correlation it is not possible to claim this as such with this size of sample / number of interviewees / though this might indicate correlation in this sample, more data would be needed to see if this reflected the characteristics of a larger population / appear to be close correlates / pseudo correlates – i.e. they appear to be at first glance but aren't if you consider another third factor

Curvilinear – this is most usually used to mean a U-shaped or upside-down U-shaped relationship. So, the relationship between A and B is positive (or negative)

up to a point, then changes, then returns to positive (or negative). You can use the same terms to qualify this that you would use in the paragraph immediately above.

Finding evidence of curvilinearity is quite rare at UG and M-Level but if you can show you can identify the possibility that a relationship might be curvilinear this is almost certain to impress readers.

Here are examples of potentially curvilinear relationships:

> Predicting a U-shape. Employee Tenure and Sales – new sales people might be especially enthusiastic and exceed their targets – particularly if there is a probation period; those who are very high performers might be with the company a very long time; people somewhere in the middle might be "solid but not spectacular".

> Predicting an upside-down U-shape. Innovations and Profitability – companies that generate no innovations may not be profitable, and perhaps those that generate a great many are not focused or precise enough about how they innovate; there might be a "sweet spot".

Now let's take these exact same examples of curvilinear relationships and turn things upside down. This is just to help you think how you might bring curvilinearity into a discussion:

> Predicting an upside-down U-shape. Employee tenure and Sales – new sales people might be enthusiastic, but they may not know the job well enough yet to make many sales; those who have been with the company a very long time might lack the necessary knowledge of the product or not be able to connect with the target market; people somewhere in the middle might be at the peak of their powers.

> Predicting a U shape. Innovations and Profitability – companies that generate no innovations may not be innovative but could be ruthlessly focused on competing on cost and therefore very profitable; perhaps those that generate a great many innovations are better able to differentiate themselves from the competition or can establish an innovative brand; meanwhile, those who are neither innovating massively nor focusing on cost may find they are in fierce competition.

Here are ways you can talk about there being opposition, conflict or tension between two nouns.

> **Strong opposition** - Dialectically opposed / diametrically opposed / antinomies / polar opposites / two poles / divorced from each other / binary opposites / paradoxical / incoherent / irreconcilable / incongruent / exclusive / mutually exclusive

> **Weaker opposition** - In tension / conflicting / conflictual / running counter to each other / somewhat in tension / divergent / inconsistent / not compatible

A relationship between two nouns where they are very closely linked, to the extent one is defined in terms of the other, or they each depend on one another. An example might be the strength of a leader and the strength of support from their followers.

> **Closely linked** - Mutually constituted / relationally enacted / interrelated / inter-defined / defined in relation to one another / co-created / co-produced / co-constituted / congruent / A entails B / A implies B / A necessitates B / without A there would be no B / A follows almost

> axiomatically from B / to say "A" is almost to imply "B"

A relationship between two nouns where they overlap but are different. An example might be job satisfaction and organizational commitment.

> **Overlap but different** - Overlapping / contiguous (strictly not an overlap but consecutive) / interlinked / convergent / family resemblance / compatible / speak to the same concerns / common roots

A relationship between two nouns where one includes the other. An example might be pay satisfaction, which is one part of job satisfaction.

> **One includes the other** - Includes / is inherent / contains within / a facet of / a component of / an aspect of / encompasses / subsumes / incorporates / contains the seeds of

Remember it's unlikely you will find enough evidence to make strong claims. This is partly because a lot of questions are answered by "it depends". It is also because you won't have time to collect much data.

This means that you would usually need to qualify whatever claims you make about their being a relationship by mentioning the scale of your study, the limited characteristics of your sample.

You might use phrases such as:

> **Qualifying findings** - based on these findings / extrapolating from these findings / it is hard to generalise / seem to be / appear to be / indicative of / some indication of / suggestive of / clearly more data would be needed to support stronger claims / the sample size provides only a limited basis for generalization / we might tentatively claim / even with a comparatively small number of interviewees, common themes suggest / potentially

Layout and Presentation

- Make sure there is enough white space on the page.
- This enhances readability and reduces reader fatigue. If your supervisor is marking several projects, make sure yours is one of those with a good layout.
- If you have more than about 300 words on a page (with no diagrams and figures of course) this may be too much.
- Use at least a 12-point font.
- Consider double spacing the main body of text.
- Have spaces after headers.
- Double space the references section and have a space after each paragraph (i.e. after each reference).
- Do it subtly and you could make it look like you have more references.

Using Quotes and Extracts

If you are presenting direct quotes or extracts and they are going to be longer than 2 lines (approximately), indent them single spaced and introduce them with a colon.

So, it would look something like this:

> Here is a quote that is longer than a couple of sentences. The advantage of setting it out in this way is that it makes it clear it is a quote, it breaks up the text and makes it easier to read. Be mindful that these sections might be read more carefully so be sure that it is relevant and well chosen.

Some tips on using quotes and extracts. Very often what you find is people choose what they think is the perfect quote or extract to illustrate a point and they conclude a paragraph or section with it. It's as if the quote is self-standing.

Instead what you often need to do is make it clear why the quote or extract is relevant and show to the reader that you can explain its significance.

It's almost like when you are working out the answer to an equation you are told to show your working – the right answer isn't enough you need to show you got there.

This is particularly important if you are presenting quotes from an interviewee, because that often requires some additional interpretation.

Below is an example:

> 1 However, at the front line, chaos and noise compromise communication. Anthony explained how the nature of leadership changed during riot situations:
>
>> Leadership becomes very tactile, words of command aren't necessarily given it's more pushes and shoves, the noise, you have to be very, very hands-on. You have to be quite autocratic [but] I'd hate to give an order and it be followed blindly. The opportunity to arrest is always there.
>
> 2 However, at the front line, chaos and noise compromise communication. Anthony explained how the nature of leadership changed during riot situations:
>
>> Leadership becomes very tactile, words of command aren't necessarily given it's more pushes and shoves, the noise, you have to be very, very hands-on. You have to be quite autocratic [but] I'd hate to give an order and it be followed blindly. The opportunity to arrest is always there.
>
> This is significant because it shows how even in situations that might seem to be purely about command and control,

> there is a need to retain individual responsibility.

In 2 just by including a short following phrase, which ties back to the theoretical understanding of leadership, the quote is analysed and put into a wider context. Just this small addition reads better.

Just as with a quote, whenever you are using an image from someone – a framework or model - see if you can develop it in some way, perhaps add a column that is more on your context or another box and arrow.

That way you can attribute it as "Based on Smith and Jones, 2008, extended to illustrate challenges of this context" or similar. This shows clearly you are applying a model, not just copy-pasting it.

If English is not your First Language

Here are the ingredients for success in writing:

- Read work of the highest quality
- Practise writing (practise, practise, practise!)
- Get quality feedback on your writing
- Revise

Speak English at every opportunity, including with people who share your first language.

To improve your vocabulary and use of English listen to quality broadcasters. The single best programme that has helped my students is Radio 4's "The Today Programme". You can hear some clips here: https://www.bbc.co.uk/programmes/b006qj9z/clips

You won't follow it all but if you re-listen these will improve your vocabulary and listening skills.

You might find this book helpful: Glasman-Deal, H. (2010). *Science research writing for non-native speakers of English*. World Scientific.

Often if you are writing in a second language you might find yourself working on getting an individual sentence perfect (to you) before moving on to write the next one.

This can make the text seem broken up.

To fix this, think about how sentences flow into one another.

The examples below are taken from the paper: Bower, J. R. (2011). Four principles to help non-native speakers of English write clearly. *Fisheries Oceanography*, 20(1), 89-91.

A☐☐ Our study site was the Bay of Bengal. Seven species of fishes were collected in the bay. Three major groups of zooplankton were fed on by the fishes. Copepods were the most abundant zooplankton prey. Euphausiids and chaetognaths composed the other prey.

B☐☐ Our study site was the Bay of Bengal. In the bay, we collected seven species of fishes. The fishes fed on three major groups of zooplankton. The most abundant zooplankton prey were copepods. The other prey comprised euphausiids and chaetognaths.

The linking phrases in example B make the sentences flow. It isn't necessary to do this with every sentence but used well it can help with fluency.

You could consider getting a copyeditor to work through a chapter of your work, or even the whole thing. Copyeditors can help you identify recurring errors.

Try to find someone who will read through your work who does speak English as their First Language.

Though your supervisor will help you correct grammatical and spelling mistakes you are going to be wasting her time if she must do this. You want her time to be spent reading your work and engaging with your ideas, not correcting mistakes.

Remember that you should be getting credit for your ideas not your expression. But if the way you express yourself is difficult to understand you can't get credit.

Part 4: Troubleshooting

"The secret of getting ahead is getting started. The secret of getting started is breaking your complex, overwhelming tasks into small manageable tasks, then starting on the first one."

Mark Twain

4 Myths about Your Thesis or Dissertation

There are plenty of myths associated with doing a Dissertation. These myths can be harmful because although they might have some truth, they are extremely unhelpful if you believe they are wholly (or even largely) true. If you don't recognise the dangers of these myths, you will not have realistic expectations which will make you less effective and is likely to lead to disappointment.

At best these slow you down, at worst they become excuses for not finishing. If you believe in them, you avoid trying to find more helpful behaviours (for example forcing yourself to write something, no matter what it looks like at first). In the worst-case scenario, they may be a justification for why you 'can't' do a Dissertation (when you actually can).

Believing in some of these myths is actually convenient at one level, because it means you aren't responsible for delays, or for failing to finish, but it is a real problem if finishing is what you really want. Everyone who completes any Dissertation has doubts at some stage: e.g. 'they must have let me in by mistake'; 'everyone else doing one is cleverer than me' etc. Below are some common myths, as well as counterarguments to each of them. You may find it useful to think about whether these or similar myths may be holding you back.

Myth 1 - You Need To Be A Genius to Do Well

Why Is This Dangerous > It's An Impossible Standard To Live Up To!

Counter > Many, many people have done projects like yours whether it's an Undergraduate degree or a PhD. It is not possible that they are all 'geniuses' (whatever that means anyway).

You are going to be following a fairly systematic procedure applied to many different people and the quality of the work that passes varies (look at some finished projects).

Myth 2 - You Have To Do Something No-One Has Ever Done Before.

Why Is This Dangerous > This Misunderstands The Nature Of A Thesis or Dissertation.

Counter > What you need do to do well is build on other people's work in a rigorous, precise way - you have to do this or else how are you adding to the existing state of knowledge? If no-one has done anything like what you're studying before then maybe it's not such a great idea! Of course what you do has to be your own work and it is original and new in that sense, but one common problem is overestimating what 'counts' as a contribution to knowledge. Precisely what that means is something you need to work on with your supervisor but reading finished projects is the best starting point.

Myth 3 - This Is Going To Be Your Life's Work And A Masterpiece Or It Will Be The Best Thing You Ever Do.

Why Is This Dangerous > Like Myth 1, It's An Impossible Standard To Reach.

Counter > Remember when you are doing a Thesis or Dissertation you are learning (by definition). The idea of a masterpiece may be helpful if you think of it as an 'apprenticeship' - i.e. when you've finished you should be ready to start as a professional researcher (for a PhD) or you are qualified as an expert in some way (for a Masters or UG degree).

But - if you stop and try to get a longer term perspective - it's actually quite discouraging to think it will be your best work (though it may be your longest). For one thing, one of the things you learn is how you could have done it better and how you would improve in future projects (All PhD students get asked a version of that question at their viva).

Myth 4 – This Will Revolutionise Or Shake The Foundations Of Your Discipline.

Why Is This Dangerous > Like Myth 2 This Misunderstands What Is Required. You Need To Finish A Time-Bound Project, Not Win A Nobel Prize.

Counter > This myth is more common to PhD students. I always tell them that you have to do what a competent PhD student could do in 3-4 years (doesn't sound so bad put like that does it?). As a PhD student it is a nice and noble intellectual dream to think you can change the way the academic community thinks because of your research.

The last thing I would want to do is discourage anyone from having dreams or from thinking big. However, if you think you have to do that in order to be awarded a

PhD you are wrong, plain and simple. Most genuinely ground-breaking research comes after not during people's PhDs.

You left it Late to Start - Now what?

The first, most important thing to do is not to panic. The second important thing you need to do is to make sure that you do make the fullest use of the time left available.

That includes not wasting time telling yourself you should have started and that you have left it to late. The same principles throughout this book apply. The following, "things can change" section can really help you.

Third, work out exactly how much time you have left and see if it is possible to negotiate more using whatever the appropriate University procedures are.

Now, go and stand in front of a mirror and say to yourself "I can do this" and "I am going to make it". It may feel silly at first but say it like you mean it and repeat this exercise regularly.

Do a table with two columns, in the left-hand column write down the contents page, in the right-hand column the % of time left you will allocate to this.

Make sure that even though you will have to work intensively, you take breaks and get fresh air and exercise and appropriate nutrition.

Coffee and chocolate (for example) feel like they are working but are only effective over a short period and the crashes you experience outweigh that temporary benefit. Caffeine can make you think you are being more productive and creative, rather than making you more productive and creative. Drinking water and having plenty of fresh fruit is a much more sustainable approach.

You are Struggling to get Access

It may not be a good use of time to chase and chase people who are not helping you and that time may be spent more wisely.

Keep an activity log of each time you try to negotiate access, so that if needed you can show you tried. Each of these could legitimately be described as contacted, and even if you had the briefest of phone calls, you spoke to someone.

What other sources of data are publicly available that you can use – annual statements, company reports, other company data, information on the market, or on the sector, the websites, competitor information?

Hard as it might be, it is much better to come up with good theoretical reasons for your final research design than it is to blame questions that are to do with practicalities and access.

Think about this argument for a design based on documentary data: I chose to focus on several sources of documentary data because this allowed for a better basis for comparison with... (similar organizations, or similar settings, or it allowed a cross-national comparison).

That is much better than this argument: because I couldn't get anyone to speak to me I looked at their website and their competitors' websites.

Problems gaining access might mean changing your research question and topic slightly – instead of an in-depth study you are looking more at competitive positioning or taking an industry rather than company focus for instance.

One of the better arguments for gaining access to some organization or setting is that you are going to be able to offer them something for free which they wouldn't otherwise get the time or resources to do.

They might not have the time for any number of projects that could help them, but you can also try to make something of your unique perspective – as an outsider looking in you could offer them something no-one in their setting, who is already embedded in that culture could see.

Think about your gatekeepers – the people who will make or break your access. They will tend to be concerned about two main things.

1. Are you going to take up a lot of their time?
2. Are you going to make them look stupid?

They will also be concerned that you should be able to offer something valuable of course, but these two considerations are what you might call "hygiene factors" or very basic needs. Keep in mind these two hygiene factors.

When you approach people make it clear you will respect their time and that any investment in time they make will have a clear payoff.

Show that you have planned the conversation beforehand. Also assure them of your professionalism in how you speak and dress. Treat initial conversations as if they were job interviews.

When you talk about your work refer to it as a "Business Project" or something that is similarly impactful. Don't talk about it as something you "have to do" that is "for your degree".

Talk about it as a rich and exciting opportunity to address real-world problems. More importantly try to avoid saying "I" but instead talk about you, your organization, benefits to you, sharing learning and so on.

Be clear about what the outputs will be. They won't want to read your work in detail. They may be interested in a focused summary with actionable recommendations. They may want a rich picture or an outsider's view. They may like a well produced vodcast.

Be very mindful of how your work may be used – does it criticise anyone, could it cause anyone harm or embarrassment? The ethics of research is not just about how you collect data you also need to be mindful of the implications of any final report.

You Haven't Got Enough Survey Responses

Be honest about what has happened in your written work

Remember at UG or M-Level you are not expected to be doing fully professional work, but you are learning about the craft of research

There are often are setbacks like this in research

You can salvage this if you:

Contact your supervisor, explain the problem

But BEFORE you do that think about what you are going to say and make sure that you can say what your plan is to ensure the work is still of the highest quality.

Say that you plan to:

- Think through more rigorously the design and methodology and to explain how what you have done could make a useful contribution as a pilot study
- Show all the different ways that you have learned from this as a pilot

- Set out what things a fuller study would need to do (and that these things would most likely be beyond scope anyway)
- Come up with a good explanation for the low response rate – audience, medium, layout, look and feel, seems old-fashioned, needs to be device agnostic (phone and PC), length, survey fatigue amongst this kind of respondents, inability to provide incentives, concerns about confidentiality, perhaps it should be administered in person not remotely, timing
- Here is a potentially great explanation – you are going to be able to say one of these: either it needs more company buy-in (which would require more care and time that a fuller project would allow); or people need to be assured it won't be linked back to the company (which would require more care over confidentiality and more careful negotiation over access)
- Describe the kinds of tests that would have been possible (do this quite quickly in a table or it can get very repetitive very quickly)
- Think about other sources of data that may be relevant (documentary data, web sites, reports, other studies)

Your Interviewee Didn't Turn Up

There is no getting away from it, this is not a good situation. Unlike with a low response survey – which can be reframed as a pilot study, there is not much you can do if you plan an interview and the person does not show. The best cure for this is not to be in this situation in the first place.

Remember that unless you can offer a tangible benefit to your interviewees or to the company you are researching, it is likely that you are entirely relying on people's good will. A lot of people do have this and may well be kind to you but let us be honest – this is not the only thing you want to count on when organising interviews.

One of the best things you can do to guard against no-shows is make some brief contact with each interviewee beforehand. Keep things very simple and short as well as friendly – beginning by thanking them for taking part is a good start. Ending by saying you look forward to meeting them is a good finish. The basic principle here is if you ask someone to confirm before you go ahead there is a much better chance someone will show.

If you can, try to link your project to their needs somehow. Maybe in return for speaking to you, you can also offer to share some of the latest ideas from your project that you think will be relevant to their area of expertise. This may help them keep up to date with the latest thinking. Or they may be able to tell you why these theories are wrong of course.

Another way of encouraging people to take part is to imply that lots of other people are doing interviews with you as well and so you could create the feeling that they wouldn't want to be the ones left out. You can also (if it is accurate) create the impression that your project has really caught the attention of someone much more senior in the organization.

Another approach is to make the person you are speaking to feel important. This is not trying to trick someone – because after all, they absolutely are important to you!

Remember too that if you have thought about the design of your project you should be able to explain to them why they are so important that you really need to speak to them.

One thing to remember is the person who has agreed you can do interviews (the "gatekeeper") may well not be there when you meet the people they have lined you up to speak with.

If they are there to introduce you of course this can be great, but it may not happen, and your interviewees may know much less about what you are doing than the gatekeeper.

Just because you have explained your project to one person in a company it does not mean others know about it.

This is another reason it is good to make initial contact with people where you can, and to offer to answer any questions they might have in advance.

If you have gone somewhere in search of interviews, but these don't take place you have a few choices.

You can choose to reconnect with the same people, try to arrange to interview different people, try a different firm or look for different data sources.

Sometimes interviews can be hard to arrange because they mean that people must be available – they are quite "invasive". As an alternative, if you can identify several sources of documentary data these have the advantage of being there before your study and all you need to do is be given access to them.

However, at the same time these kinds of data are also often quite thin pieces of information (unless you have a very large company). Reports and minutes or company leaflets and magazines are not always in the same depth and detail.

One thing you may need to do if you are struggling to get people to talk to is to broaden out the scope of your study. It may be easier to change the research question slightly and to broaden the scope. For instance, if you intended to look at a company you might need to rethink and then look at a sector.

Alternatively (see the section "Things can Change") you might need to make more drastic changes.

The advantage of looking at a sectoral or industry level is that any documentary data you find may be something that applies to several different firms.

Things can Change

Here is a good thing to remember that can perhaps be most useful if your plans for getting data or agreeing access fall through.

This is a difficult thing to do and it is unlike any other exam or assignment you will have done. However, one beauty of doing this project is: you get to write the question.

Not only that, you get to write the question after you have finished your answer. Remember that – with your supervisor's agreement - you can always change your topic and title.

Something you may have heard as a student is that a common problem with some assessed work (particularly exams) is that it doesn't answer the question set. With you this should never happen because you get to choose what the question is.

The reason that change can be a problem is that sometimes students feel they must stick to an original plan (and title) and no matter what happens as they progress they must try to fit circumstances around that original plan.

Remember that things are not necessarily going to go to plan. In a PhD you might have time to address that and change things, so they do go back to plan. At UG or M-Level you may well not have time to do this.

Your first proposal or plan is not fixed and it may even need to change.

In the course of what you are doing, you can change: the title, the topic area, the question, the main subject, the method.

However, you need to do what you can to make sure your supervisor is ok with your doing this, and that you can provide good reasons for that.

At the very least you need to advise them of having made any significant changes so that when it comes to their marking your work it is not a surprise.

Also, think about the reasons you give and the case you make when you ask them to agree to or accept your changes.

Stop Procrastinating – Yes... You Can!

This is a very common and important concern for people. Here are 4 suggestions / ideas. First though, ask yourself this question – do you feel you could do some work on your project right now? If you answered yes, go and do it then come back to this section when you need a break.

<u>"Procrastinating"</u>

Here is the first suggestion: *avoid* using this general label to think about your behaviour or your results. Eliminate this word from your vocabulary. Instead, try to think much more specifically about what is happening *with you* at *particular times* with *particular tasks* in relation to *particular goals*.

The problem with the label is we can tell ourselves the reason that we didn't do something is "because" we were procrastinating or "because" we are a terrible procrastinator. But this is a trick we are playing on ourselves. There isn't a "because" - this label doesn't help to explain anything or give us any insight. For instance, look at this dialogue:

> Sanjay "Oh mate I'm such a procrastinator!"
> Debs "Oh no way! Me too! I'm really terrible for procrastinating!"
> Sanjay "Bet you're not as bad as me!"

Debs "Bet you that I am!"
etc. etc.

All this is doing is using a very generic label to try to justify why we have less than desirable outcomes. The problem is this label becomes "the reason" we haven't done what we wanted to. It then becomes an excuse or a stick we beat ourselves with making everything feel worse.

Let's try this – say to yourself you are no longer a procrastinator or someone who procrastinates – find another way of talking about why you aren't achieving your goals.

Goals and Tasks

Here is the second suggestion: it really can help if you make your goals more specific. This is helped by planning at the start of the day what you want to accomplish. As already mentioned, people often say something like "I'm going to spend today on my literature review". That can work but often isn't sustainable because it's too big a task and it's not a realisable goal in a day. If you break your project into smaller tasks and goals that can be helpful.

Another related consideration is the nature of the task. Some tasks require high skill and are highly challenging, it might be you are the kind of person who needs to "warm up" before taking these on. Or you could be the kind of person who needs to do these first while you have most energy.

If you have more specific goals (e.g. find 20 relevant articles / read 5 articles / write 600 words on a topic / learn more about the aims and scope of 5 journals / work out how many words needed in each section of my project) you can schedule tasks in ways that suit you. Tick them off when they are done as it feels good. That can also help build momentum - if you exceed your day's goals then great.

Displacement

Here is the third suggestion: Freud identified a number of defence mechanisms, one of which relevant to writing was displacement. These defence mechanisms are how the subconscious prevents our conscious mind – the ego – from sources of threat or anxiety (simplifying his model). They are often less than ideal ways of coping with problems because they lead to distraction and never address the issue head on.

The most typical example given of displacement is where we take out anger or frustration on an object other than the one causing us to be angry or frustrated. If your boss is annoyingly incompetent or even bullying you, you may take this out on other "safer" targets – unknowingly picking an argument with a friend for instance.

Where displacement becomes relevant in a project is a bit more subtle than this. There are many tasks associated with doing a project and sometimes people displace activity from one to another.

If you find it really hard to think how to write your conclusion for example you might say to yourself "I'll just polish up my methods section". But then the problem with displacement may be this is all you end up doing in a day – so you actually just put something off.

Another really common displacement phenomenon which is even more subtle is when people spend too much time preparing and never actually starting – they might spend ages tidying up their room for example.

Activation Energy

Here is the fourth idea: first though, please let me ask again – do you feel you could do some work on your project right now? If you can, go and do it NOW then come back to this section when you need a break.

Activation energy refers to the will to do something – to get up, make a phone call, to go for a run, get changed, do some work etc. Some people have suggested that once you have decided you are going to do something you have around 5 seconds before this energy runs out.

There's a simple lesson here – if you feel like doing something that can move your project forward, make sure you act on it before that energy fizzles out and you find yourself distracted or following other impulses.

Here's a hack relating to activation energy that you might find helpful. If you take the example of going for a run, then you probably have experienced how activation energy can dissipate if you have to find things like your socks, water bottle and trainers.

If you wander round looking for these things you may get distracted and lose momentum so – well in advance - make sure all the things that you need to go for a run are in one place and easy to access.

To apply this to your project - really work hard on your morning routine. If you get the first hour right it helps so much. And also start this the night before writing a 2-3 minute plan for the day.

Major Changes: How to Tell Your Supervisor

First think about this hierarchy of reasons that you could give for having to change your plans: practical, methodological and theoretical. It applies to thinking about changing your project, it also applies more widely.

It is better for you if you can try to think about academic or theoretical reasons for any changes. If you do this, you are going to keep at the front of your mind the criteria by which your work is eventually evaluated.

When it comes to evaluating someone's work, academics are more impressed by theoretical justifications (and reasons for changes) than any others. They are not as impressed by reasons that are to do with the practical difficulties of doing research.

Any supervisor who has carried out research themselves will not need to be told about how it can be hard to get people to speak to you or how it can be hard to get a decent number of responses to a survey.

Even if you were doing just a review you need to think carefully if you ever give a reason for not having done something. Supervisors know if a lot has been written about a topic for example, and they don't need to be told that reading all the literature on a topic is not possible.

At the same time, that would not be a good excuse for missing out a very influential theory or author.

Compare these three examples. This shows different ways of explaining to a supervisor why it was not possible to carry out interviews as originally planned.

Only Practical	Practical & Methodological	Practical, Theoretical & Methodological
Dear ... Hope you are well. Apologies for writing, I know you are very busy. It was just a quick note to share an update, and specifically a change to my planned methods and data.

It has not been possible to carry out the planned interviews | Dear ... Hope you are well. Apologies for writing, I know you are very busy. It was just a quick note to share an update, and specifically a change to my planned methods and data.

It has not been possible to carry out the planned interviews because getting access has proved difficult.

Instead my plan is to focus more on | Dear ... Hope you are well. Apologies for writing, I know you are very busy. I just wanted to share a suggested slight change of direction with you because if this is not a good plan it would be better to know now. Happy to discuss this if helpful.

I have been facing some problems because it is proving extremely difficult to arrange access to interviewees as originally planned. But having reflected on this I think this could open up |

because getting access has proved difficult. Please could I meet with you to discuss a way forward?	documentary analysis using data in the public domain. To make this extensive enough to allow for in depth analysis my plan is also to look more at industry level rather than at the level of one company. This means I will need to change my plans but am still on course to finish on time...	an opportunity and lead to a more interesting project. Now that I'm familiar with a lot more of the literature I think there may be an exciting opportunity to try to say something new by looking more carefully at existing secondary data sources. This would involve refocusing slightly to use data in the public domain. To make this extensive enough to allow for in depth analysis my plan is to look more at industry level rather than at the level of one company...

The example in the third column is more impressive. It makes – even only briefly - reference to the academic literature and it sounds well organised. It communicates that the person has been trying but is also flexible and interested in what they are doing.

It also suggests a reason that it is difficult to argue with – they want to change things because they know what will be a more interesting project having done more reading – how could they have known this at the proposal stage?

A good, theoretical justification for change, combined with practicalities, is always going to carry more weight than purely practical reasons.

A likely response to this 3rd column email would be the Supervisor is fine with this plan and doesn't need to meet.

Think about Your 'Wins'

Your Supervisor will be more worried about people who do not keep them up to date and have just disappeared without warning, or they will be having their patience tested by those students who are constantly asking them questions which they should be deciding for themselves.

Here, there is a clear justification for the student to have contacted them, and the student has not just contacted them with a problem but with a solution (also a good strategy for you to pursue in your professional life with anyone who is managing you).

Keep in mind they may look much more favourably on changes they were kept up to date with.

A small tactical point here, is that by offering the chance to discuss the suggested change with them, it then becomes difficult for the Supervisor to suggest that you didn't do what was agreed.

When they later evaluate this person's work they will know what to expect and they will have been consulted.

Notice the difference between an approach that is "can we meet to discuss this please" and "here is my plan, what do you think, I'm happy to discuss this". Obviously in the second approach you are showing the ability to work independently.

Think about what the wins are for you here. It might feel like a victory if you manage to insist on a meeting with your supervisor and you get them to agree to what you do.

But that isn't necessarily a win for your supervisor – particularly if they feel things could have gone ahead without a meeting or if they feel they are being bossed around ("managing your supervisor" is certainly not about showing your supervisor that you are the 'real' boss).

They will be more impressed with someone who contacts them only occasionally, with a clear plan in mind, who only contacts them when necessary and after care, and who only does that after showing they have planned how to use their time to work independently.

If you have some questions you feel you need to ask your supervisor, wait a few days if you can before you contact them. It is much, much better to send one email with 4 questions than 4 emails each with one question.

Masterclass - 20 Examples of Successful Research

This table shows examples of successful research – where there has been a **PROBLEM** or question, there has been a certain kind of **RESEARCH**, leading to **IMPLICATIONS**

PROBLEM	RESEARCH	IMPLICATIONS
Supermarkets wanted to understand the needs of their customers with allergies better	Researchers followed people in their homes using the technique of observation – this is a form of realist ethnography	They found people had a separate allergen-free section in their fridge – so they reorganised stores to have "Free from" sections
A niche e-retailer of 2nd hand agricultural machinery is looking to expand - should they open a new office in China or India?	This is a question about "market entry" - research could involve applying strategic tools to evaluate the strengths of the firm and potential of the market (5 forces, SWOT, RBV, sources of competitive advantage,	A researcher with dedicated time might be able to reveal that there are fundamental differences between the markets in these two countries/regions – e.g. one is maybe more of a 'buyers' market' one is more a

	competitive context etc)	'seller's market'
What is it like to work here? what are we like as a company? – a firm wants to understand these questions better because they can be a source of advantage – or disadvantage	Sometimes outsiders to a firm can answer these questions more easily, or at least give a different perspective because these are questions about culture – which is often to do with assumptions that are never questioned (a "cultural audit")	Firms could find out any number of things by asking this – for example an outsider might make them aware that one of their habits (going for a drink after work) was indirectly discriminatory because in some cultures and religions, alcohol is prohibited
Before launching a new flavour of a food or drink companies want to know if it will sell so they test the product	Product testing is an example of research that is based on the same logic of sampling which you often find in survey designs (for example hiding the brand so people don't know whether they are tasting the original formula or a	Sometimes firms identify improvements to a formulation, other times this kind of research can have surprising results – for instance showing that the brand itself (packaging) has an effect on people's

	new version)	perceptions
To evaluate the effectiveness of the positioning of product on supermarket shelves – where is the "premium" shelf space	People used to believe the premium location was at eye-level. Eye mark recording shows that people actually tend to spend more time browsing products that are below eye level	This changed the pricing strategies for supermarkets instore and also the marketing mix (positioning) for companies trying to sell their brands
What things does an organization have to work on to remain profitable? What things do we need to learn or what skills do we need to develop?	This could be described as a "needs assessment" – a researcher could gather information about existing processes and practices, identify areas for training or growth using strategic tools (SWOT and those above) and benchmarking (balanced	This could identify changes needed in recruitment or training, or reward systems – or more external facing functions like marketing and communications, or customer service

	scorecard)	
The pharmaceutical company Boots wanted to understand more about its corporate history because it was looking for a way to measure its brand value more accurately - to make it more resistant to takeover	Boots has an unusual resource, a company archive storing materials going back over 100 years (newsletters, old adverts, leaflets and company documents, relevant policy) a researcher did a historical analysis of these documents	They could describe several stages in Boots' history (the 19th Century, Boots in the pre-second world war period, Boots after the NHS etc.) and they showed that while some things had changed a lot over time Boots also had a continuing corporate identity and strong Corporate Social Responsibility strand in this identity, which was an important part of its culture
Are recruitment and selection processes biased in terms of race or gender?	Researchers have carried out real life experiments where they have applied to the same jobs, with identical CVs	This has been done more than once and the effects are disturbing because they show that people from dominant

	but changed the name of the applicant so that in one case it is from the dominant ethnic group and in a second case it is from a minority.	ethnic groups can be more likely to be invited for interview than people from minority communities. There can also be gender effects.
Companies like Google and Amazon exploit something called "base erosion" – they pay much less tax than would be suggested by the amount of economic activity they generate	After interviewing different stakeholders (tax officials, company representatives, accountants) a researcher showed how there was a problem in how accounting practices evaluate economic activity	Companies can exploit legislation to avoid paying tax on economic activity by re-defining the source and value of this activity. So, even if Amazon sells 10s of millions of items in the UK, they can argue that the value of the business is not in selling books or electronic goods, but that it is a logistics company whose advantage lies in Intellectual Property that is generated in the US or low tax areas. This has

		implications for CSR and the relationship between MNCs and the Nation State.
A researcher wanted to understand the differences in power between nurses and doctors in a large hospital	He worked in the hospital as a Doctor and watched how people behaved over a long period of observation. He found that there was a room which was informally only for nurses – doctors never went in there even though this was never written down as policy anywhere.	This showed the simple picture people have – that doctors were always more powerful than nurses - was wrong. There were different ways in which nurses could be powerful – by showing they had control and ownership of this space. It also suggested that they needed a room to go in to "decompress" or simply to get away from doctors.
A government agency wanted to save money by spending less on elderly care	By interviewing different stakeholders (elderly people, staff in care	They might find that some relatively inexpensive changes –

and needed to understand how multiple agencies worked together	homes, staff in hospitals, community visitors, nursing staff, housing officials) a researcher might get more of an all-round or a holistic perspective on this problem	modifying people's houses to make them less likely to fall – could lead to fewer accidents and hospital admissions.
Researchers wanted to improve employee retention in a large accountancy firm. Reducing turnover would save sizable sums of money.	Most people had researched employee turnover by asking people what things might make them think of leaving (perhaps they were dissatisfied with their pay). These researchers asked people after they had left why they had left.	They found that many of the reasons people quit a job could not be predicted. Instead there were often unexpected or family reasons. Also, sometimes people clashed with their supervisor and so this suggested ways to manage turnover more effectively.
The Hawthorne Works Electric company wanted to know what working	Researchers chose one group of workers and altered things like the lights,	They concluded that it was because this group was being observed - made

conditions made their workers more effective	the position of the desks, work patterns and found something surprising – whatever changes were made, this group was observed to have improved performance.	to feel different and special that mattered, not the changes themselves. This became known as the Hawthorne effect and revolutionised approaches to management.
Amway a network marketing organisation was very effective at inducting new members – how?	One researcher became an Amway distributor and whilst working there he noticed that the company was outstanding at establishing a sense of organizational identification. In other words, they gave people very clear answers to the question "what does it mean to work at Amway"	The researcher described this process as being in two parts - one of "sense-breaking" and one of "sense-giving" Amway first broke down people's existing ideas about identity and what it meant to belong to an organization. Then they remade that identity by creating a very powerful, idealised image of what Amway was and did. Almost like a

		cult.
What happens when people agree to do a task and then part-way through the terms of the task change – for instance they say they will get less than originally agreed? Why do they keep going and how do they feel about it?	This is a very interesting effect that has been seen in real life and also studied using a lot of lab and experimental studies (playing games with participants and changing the rules midway). The surprising thing is that people can continue with a task and find it even *more* interesting if part-way through the terms change and they are paid less.	What is going on? Well researchers call this the paradigm of "insufficient justification". Basically, the explanation for this is that to reduce ongoing dissatisfaction at being paid unfairly, people will try to compensate somehow by finding the task more intrinsically rewarding. Rather than carrying on and feeling unhappy – people will often find another reason to enjoy the task and "cognitively restructure" it.
What effects do race and gender biases have on customer	Researchers carried out a number of laboratory studies and also	This has some huge implications in terms of corporate social

| satisfaction? | surveys to evaluate whether there were separate effects because of gender or race on customer satisfaction. The disturbing evidence from some of these studies is that customers' ratings of satisfaction are affected by the race or gender of the people providing them with a service, independent of the quality of the service. | responsibility and the prevailing rhetoric of the customer always being right. Perhaps most immediately it suggests that race and gender effects should always be taken account of when evaluating people in terms of ratings of customer satisfaction. Bonuses or even disciplinary outcomes may not be valid reflections of service quality. Customers are not – obviously – trained to understand and overcome unconscious bias so why should an employee's performance ratings be in their hands? |
| How important | A researcher | A very surprising |

is trust in acquisition of entrepreneurial firms?	showed how acquisitions of entrepreneurial firms are characterised by asymmetries in terms of trust. Buyers (those looking to acquire firms) and sellers (firms themselves) have very different views about deception and take different actions to avoid deception.	finding is that selecting buyers on the basis of trust (rather than other commercial factors) can actually increase the risk to entrepreneurial firms. This is because buyers and sellers often have erroneous views about trust
What makes some people more successful in their careers than others?	Researchers surveyed people and mapped out their networks – looking at the kinds of resources they could access in terms of their network, and the overall shape and structure of their network (how big it was, whether it was	They develop an explanation for career success in terms of social capital. Over and above people's on the job abilities, their career success was dependent on the benefits their network gave them in terms of: information, resources and career

	concentrated in certain ways).	sponsorship.
Should firms expand internationally through start-ups or acquisitions?	This is quite a big question in strategy – one factor is the extent to which this choice is a function of the firm's multinational diversity and also their product diversity.	One finding has been that greater multinational diversity leads to more foreign start-ups rather than acquisitions. Product diversity has a more complicated effect on the tendency to use start-ups. At the extremes (low or high product diversity) companies are more likely to grow through start-ups.
How do you explain large scale phenomena by looking at smaller groups and relationships	One of the most cited papers in Sociology, "The Strength of Weak Ties" was a theoretical contribution. It focused on the relationship between two people - a 'dyadic tie'.	Putting an emphasis on weak ties and dyads meant this approach could be scaled up more easily to consider relations between groups and to analyse of another aspect to

	Whilst most models of networks looked at strong ties (well defined groups) this approach considered weak ties – friendships.	social structure that is not easily defined in terms of well defined groups.

Not all these studies are referenced or published, some are more general than any one study and others have multiple studies attached to them. But you can follow a lot of them up in the references section at the end.

References

Adair, J. G. (1984). The Hawthorne effect: a reconsideration of the methodological artefact. *Journal of Applied Psychology*, 69(2), 334.

Barkema, H. G., & Vermeulen, F. (1998). International expansion through start-up or acquisition: A learning perspective. *Academy of Management Journal*, 41(1), 7-26.

Graebner, M. E. (2009). Caveat venditor: Trust asymmetries in acquisitions of entrepreneurial firms. *Academy of Management Journal*, 52(3), 435-472.

Granovetter, M. S. (1973). The Strength of Weak Ties. *American Journal of Sociology*, 78(6): 1360-1380.

Lee, T. W., Mitchell, T. R., Holtom, B. C., McDaniel, L. S., & Hill, J. W. (1999). The unfolding model of voluntary turnover: A replication and extension. *Academy of Management journal*, 42(4), 450-462.

Morrell, K., Loan-Clarke, J., Arnold, J., & Wilkinson, A. (2008). Mapping the decision to quit: A refinement and test of the unfolding model of voluntary turnover. *Applied Psychology*, 57(1), 128-150.

Pfeffer, J., & Lawler, J. (1980). Effects of job alternatives, extrinsic rewards, and behavioral commitment on attitude toward the organization: A field test of the insufficient justification paradigm. *Administrative Science Quarterly*, 38-56.

Pratt, M. G. (2000). The good, the bad, and the ambivalent: Managing identification among Amway distributors. *Administrative Science Quarterly*, 45(3), 456-493.

Rowlinson, M., & Hassard, J. (1993). The invention of corporate culture: A history of the histories of Cadbury. *Human Relations*, 46(3), 299-326.

Seibert, S. E., Kraimer, M. L., & Liden, R. C. (2001). A social capital theory of career success. *Academy of Management Journal*, 44(2), 219-237.

Incidentally, below is the same list of references as above in a slightly larger font, spaced out a little. Don't overdo this but you should be able to see that it looks like more references. (Don't number your references by the way, it looks amateurish).

References

Adair, J. G. (1984). The Hawthorne effect: a reconsideration of the methodological artifact. *Journal of Applied Psychology*, 69(2), 334.

Barkema, H. G., & Vermeulen, F. (1998). International expansion through start-up or acquisition: A learning perspective. *Academy of Management Journal, 41*(1), 7-26.

Graebner, M. E. (2009). Caveat venditor: Trust asymmetries in acquisitions of entrepreneurial firms. *Academy of Management Journal, 52*(3), 435-472.

Granovetter, M. S. (1973). The Strength of Weak Ties. *American Journal of Sociology,* 78(6): 1360-1380.

Lee, T. W., Mitchell, T. R., Holtom, B. C., McDaniel, L. S., & Hill, J. W. (1999). The unfolding model of voluntary turnover: A replication and extension. *Academy of Management journal, 42*(4), 450-462.

Morrell, K., Loan-Clarke, J., Arnold, J., & Wilkinson, A. (2008). Mapping the decision to quit: A refinement and test of the unfolding model of voluntary turnover. *Applied Psychology, 57*(1), 128-150.

Pfeffer, J., & Lawler, J. (1980). Effects of job alternatives, extrinsic rewards, and behavioral commitment on attitude toward the organization: A field test of the insufficient justification paradigm. *Administrative Science Quarterly*, 38-56.

Pratt, M. G. (2000). The good, the bad, and the ambivalent: Managing identification among Amway distributors. *Administrative Science Quarterly*, 45(3), 456-493.

Rowlinson, M., & Hassard, J. (1993). The invention of corporate culture: A history of the histories of Cadbury. *Human Relations*, 46(3), 299-326.

Seibert, S. E., Kraimer, M. L., & Liden, R. C. (2001). A social capital theory of career success. *Academy of Management Journal*, 44(2), 219-237.

Masterclass For PhDs – Preparing for an Upgrade

Often an upgrade (passing your first year) involves doing a mini-viva after handing in a longish document. What a panel want to see basically is:

- whether you are on course to complete

Expressing this more specifically they will want:

- evidence that you have done some work
- evidence you have a good handle on the literature
- a well defined topic and research questions
- a good account of methods and data
- an idea about likely contribution
- identification of potential barriers or risks (like access issues or whether you have the required skills in methods)
- they will want an idea of timings too.

You can use the how to write an abstract 7-step formula both to structure your document and to prepare your presentation if you have to give one of these.

During the panel be very welcoming of criticism, but be careful not to concede too much on big points (unless the criticisms are entirely valid of course) – examples of these big points might be whether your research is feasible or whether you know the literature and are heading for a contribution or whether your methods are appropriate and whether you have the competence to carry out the methods.

If the panel says something you have thought about and you have a clear solution, then acknowledge it is a good point and something you have considered – but not in an arrogant or dismissive way. The panel do need to be able to follow your thought processes. Something you think might be obvious is not necessarily obvious to them.

If they say something important that you haven't thought about and it throws you a little, acknowledge this is something new to you and you can also thank or even compliment them, "I hadn't thought of that, it's a really good point".

This way it could seem like less of an embarrassing gap in your knowledge or preparation, and more like a conversation between professionals.

If something comes up that you don't know how to answer just say you need to think about it. Don't be too defensive or antagonistic. By the time you are physically in the room and talking a lot will have already been decided. This is because it is the written document that counts and this reflects work you have done over time.

An antagonistic attitude will go down very badly. In contrast, even if you are heading for major changes, if you are positive and constructive that will count in your favour.

If your upgrade went well you don't need help then. What if it goes badly?

When an Upgrade goes Badly

At the institutions I know of, there is always a chance to redo this mini-viva even if it goes extremely badly. You can think of it as a revise and resubmit. The first thing you need to do is get a clear steer and impression from your supervisor.

When talking about the mini viva to your supervisor(s) you should try to sound very positive about the process (without minimising the idea that it would involve a lot of work and was critical).

This will communicate to your supervisor that you are serious and have listened and learned, it will also make it easier (if you have to) to argue down the line that you responded to their comments constructively. Part of how well you do from there on is inevitably going to be about the impression you create with your supervisor. The worst thing you can do if it went badly is to try to pretend otherwise.

Be aware that you may be in shock and so if you are asked to comment you can always acknowledge it is a shock and to take more time.

Trying to make your supervisor responsible for a bad outcome is unlikely to be a good strategy because whilst you are entitled to good supervision, you are working at Doctoral level and this is an independent piece of research.

The panel will form an impression of your abilities and these will be based on your ideas, your writing and your presentation. Just like if you sent an article to a journal and you were lead author, you couldn't expect the editor or reviewers to treat you any differently because your second and third authors made mistakes or didn't contribute as much as you hoped.

Finish Your Thesis or Dissertation!

That's it! I'm not going to wish you luck because you don't need it.

1. Set your goals.
2. Focus, work hard and smart.
3. Look after yourself.

Here's a link to a playlist of 12 videos, this short series will help you consolidate learning from the book:

https://www.youtube.com/playlist?list=PL85jYxmsDS_3LFcGph3ohtWNQMnVM7NfV

Printed in Poland
by Amazon Fulfillment
Poland Sp. z o.o., Wrocław